THE CHILDREN OF ISRAEL: THE BENE ISRAEL OF BOMBAY

THE CHILDREN
OF ISRAEL:
THE BENE ISRAEL OF
BOMBAY

SCHIFRA STRIZOWER

Indian Branch
OXFORD UNIVERSITY PRESS
1971

Edition for
India, Burma, Ceylon and Nepal

First published in India by
John Brown, Oxford University Press, Bombay

Printed in Great Britain by
Western Printing Services Ltd, Bristol
and bound by Kemp Hall Bindery, Oxford

Contents

Part II

THE BENE ISRAEL AND THE WORLD BEYOND COMMUNAL BOUNDARIES

Part III

WITHIN COMMUNAL BOUNDARIES

Foreword

I am told that it is most unusual for a member of a community that is the subject of anthropological investigation to write a Foreword to the resulting book. If, therefore, this Foreword is something of an innovation in the literature of social anthropology, it is a welcome one, because what scholars record about communities ultimately passes into common currency and shapes the attitudes of ordinary people towards those communities. Dr Strizower's delineation of the social characteristics of the Bene Israel of India which identify them as Jews and those which distinguish them from Jews elsewhere, even if it circulates at first mainly in learned circles (though there is no reason why it should be so confined, seeing how free it is from esoteric jargon), is likely to influence the image of the community among fellow Indians and, more important, among Jews outside India. To have a chance to make a few comments from the receiving end is indeed fortunate.

With most of the findings in the book I entirely agree. From a few I dissent, but it is not necessary for me to indicate them, as I may well be swayed by unconscious bias. One of the points of disagreement has, however, been mentioned by Dr Strizower herself, in Note 4 to Chapter 9, p. 147, wherein my disagreement with her on the question of missionary influence on the Bene Israel at a certain stage of their history has been cited.

Dr Strizower's study is the first considerable work on the Bene Israel since the invaluable (albeit apologetic) *History of the Bene Israel of India* by H. S. Kehimkar, completed in 1897 but published only in 1937, the admirable *Jews in India and the Far East* by the Rev. H. L. Lord, published in 1907, and the article by the same author on the Bene Israel in Hasting's *Encyclopaedia of Religion and Ethics*. She was particularly fortunate in the time she chose for carrying out her field study. The picture she has drawn is of a community with its main institutions intact and in fair working order, a community with no doubts or fears about its future, a community barely conscious of the precariousness of its position. Yet, as her Conclusion suggests, the portents of radical change for the worse were already present when she gave her final touches to her study. And these have grown more ominous day by day.

The trickle of emigration, mainly to Israel, has become a flood. If emigration continues at the present rate, the Bene Israel will, within ten years or so, be reduced to a rump incapable of maintaining any significant activity as a coherent community. Coupled with emigration there is in India growing assimilation through intermarriage and conscious dissociation from Judaism on the part of those who remain.

Any future study of the Bene Israel in Bombay can only be of a community in disarray. Synagogues in the Konkan (the mainland across Bombay Harbour) are closing one by one. Those in Bombay find it difficult to obtain or retain competent Readers and one of the oldest has already discontinued daily services, holding services only on Mondays and Thursdays. Fewer congregants or even professional Readers can read the portion of the Law from the Scroll, and fewer still can give authoritative guidance in matters of ritual. Where in the past there was keen competition for places on the managing boards of synagogues and other institutions, there are today not enough candidates to fill all the seats (and yet a curious reluctance to amalgamate and consolidate resources). The co-operative lending society cannot secure enough borrowers to maintain its solvency. The School, once the pride of the community, has less than a hundred Bene Israel pupils out of a total enrolment of a thousand or so and, for some reason its report and accounts have remained unpublished for several years. The communal cemetery is in a disgraceful condition and the communal orphanage and old people's home is in the last stages of decay. What is more, few care any longer even to protest at mismanagement or worse. Nor is any effective attention paid to the alarming increase in the number of homeless destitutes who are unable to secure the aid of the Jewish Agency to migrate to Israel. To crown all, we are not even ashamed of dumping our aged and our infirm on Israel. This is a gloomy picture, but it needs to be set against any more rosy impression that may arise from Dr Strizower's description of the position only a few years ago.

As will be evident from Dr Strizower's description, the Bene Israel cannot claim to have made any significant contribution to the enrichment of the Jewish tradition. But this can be said to their credit; they refused to die out, as so many other Jewish groups did in other parts of the world less isolated from centres of World Jewry. It is true that the Hindu environment favoured survival, but the Muslims were in power for some centuries in the area and they attracted many converts, particularly from the lower castes. The Bene Israel lived in very close association with the Muslims, but were never tempted to adopt Islam. The Christian missionaries made a most determined drive to convert the Bene Israel since 1813, as will be evidenced by Dr John Wilson's tract *Appeal for the Christian Education of the Bene Israel* cited by Dr Strizower. Here the material attractions were considerable but the Bene Israel stood firm. Was it merely inertia or the influence of the Hindu concept of *Dharma* which requires every man to remain in, and fulfil the duties of, the station in which it has pleased Providence to place him? Or was it a stubborn pride in their Jewish heritage, however imperfectly perceived it may have been? Whatever it be, survival has always been very highly rated in the Jewish scale of values.

What the future holds for the Bene Israel is alarming to contemplate. Those who migrate to Israel will doubtless lose in time those peculiarities which marked them off from other Jews and will get assimilated to the general Israeli community. Those who remain in India will be under temptation to assimilate, not from any external pressure, but from inability to sustain a focus of Jewish loyalty. The Bene Israel, as such, may cease to be.

This will be a loss to India, if not to World Jewry. However insignificant a part the Bene Israel played in the general life of India, by their very existence in sizable numbers on the West Coast, they have constituted a Jewish presence in India which in its small way has enriched its multi-faceted culture. More important, they have provided living evidence that, in at least one country in the world, Jews can exist with pride and honour and without any need for self-consciousness or protective withdrawal into a self-created ghetto.

Is it not possible that the Bene Israel have been a puzzle to other Jews partly for this very reason? The image of the Jew to the Christian and the Islamic World was that of a creature living precariously at the capricious mercy of those who, where they did not hate, despised him and yet, paradoxically in Christian lands, feared him. His Jewish heritage had to be carefully guarded from external assault and the Jew became withdrawn, self centred and constantly on the defensive. The Bene Israel never had cause to fear and they, therefore, saw no danger in free intercourse with their neighbours and full participation in the life of the general community. The minutiae of Jewish observance which elsewhere served to preserve the distinct identity of the Jewish people in an alien and hostile environment could, therefore, not interest the Bene Israel. None of the traditionally Jewish occupations elsewhere, such as high finance and international trade, were entered by the Bene Israel. In fact, after they had given up their traditional occupation of oil-pressing, the Bene Israel could no longer be identified with any particular calling. It was their very 'normality' which made them such strange Jews, strange to Jews of other lands and strange to the educated Indian who derived his image of the Jew from English books. This 'normality' may be similar to that now seen in the Israeli Sabra which has the appearance of an abandonment of Judaism.

All in all Dr Strizower's book is valuable as much for the questions which arise from her descriptions and comments as for those descriptions and comments themselves. It deserves to be widely read and, in particular, to be closely studied by the Bene Israel.

Bombay,   B. J. Israel
October, 1970.

Acknowledgements

This book is based on a thesis presented for the Ph.D. degree in the University of London. I wish to thank Professor Adrian C. Mayer for the solicitude and severity with which he supervised it. This is no mere formal expression of gratitude: my debt to him for all I have learnt from him and for his untiring sympathy is much greater than I can adequately acknowledge.

I am grateful to Professor C. von Fürer-Haimendorf and Professor F. G. Bailey for gently but persistently prodding me to complete the thesis. But Professor Bailey is also the editor of this series, and I must thank him again for his great help and patience at the stage when the thesis was becoming a book.

Anyone undertaking an anthropological study of a Jewish community must be considerably indebted to Professor Maurice Freedman; but I also owe him a particular debt of gratitude for his critical comments and encouraging interest.

I must thank the Bene Israel. In spite of the misunderstandings that have arisen in the past over much that has been reported about them, they showed me great kindness, invited me to their homes, allowed me to participate in their social life, and even encouraged my curiosity. I am very grateful to Mr B. J. Israel, a member of the community, who has taken the time and the trouble to read through an earlier draft of the book and give me detailed comments which furthered my understanding of the subject.

I must add that I have occasionally plagiarized in the course of the following pages from my articles on Indian Jewry. Having once said a thing as forcibly as one is capable of saying it, I cannot see why there should be a moral obligation to vary the phraseology on future occasions.

My family was one for whom the study and practice of Judaism was the purpose of life. Almost all of them, on both my mother's side and my father's side, died in the camps of Europe for the sanctification of His name. To their memory I dedicate this book about a lesser-known Jewish community in a more hospitable country.

My field work was financed by the Department of Educational and Cultural Reconstruction of the Conference on Jewish Material Claims against Germany.

September 1970   SCHIFRA STRIZOWER

Part I
MEMORIES AND CUSTOMS

1
Introduction

Jews differ from one another in many ways. They show almost, but not quite, every physical variation that is to be found among human beings. Like Christians, different Jews belong to many different nations. Culturally they live in many different worlds.

In theory, the various Jewish communities, whatever the differences between them, are of equal status. But in practice, differences between Jewish communities tend to be accompanied by a difference in social valuation. The result is often considerable friction. For example, there used to be intense friction, amounting almost to hostility, between the German Jews and the Jews from Eastern Europe who came to settle in Germany. The former considered themselves socially superior, and the latter resented this infringement of Jewish egalitarianism. Again, prior to Indian independence the relations between the Bene Israel of Bombay and the Jews from Baghdad who came to settle in Bombay were in many ways not unlike the relations between Indians and Europeans. Bene Israel informants told me, 'Indians were a subject people; and so, because of our Indian characteristics, the Baghdadis, being fair-complexioned and tending towards a European mode of life, considered themselves superior to our Bene Israel. These fair-complexioned Jews considered themselves fit to consort with the white rulers of India. So they did not want to mix with their coloured fellow Jews but preferred to align themselves with the Europeans. Of course it was all very, very wrong—and our Bene Israel resented it.'

The world beyond the Jewish horizon—by no means as irrelevant as Judaism would make it appear to be—thus interferes with the effectiveness of common religion as a principle of unity. For the world beyond the Jewish horizon not infrequently

B

suggests other kinds of alignments, based on different principles of recruitment.

This study, concerned with the Bene Israel of Bombay, the largest Jewish community in India, looks at a problem found among all Jewish communities (and among minorities of other sorts)—where, in the larger society, they are to find their level.

But it is also about relationships within the Jewish community, about the definition of a Jew, about—of all things—ethnic prejudice between Jews—questions which have caused Bene Israel no small agony.

The Bene Israel have been something of a puzzle to their fellow Jews: they are a part of Jewry; but having been isolated for centuries from the mainstream of Jewish life and influenced by a social system not usually associated with Judaism, neither they nor their co-religionists have been able to rid themselves of the impression that Bene Israel do not belong in quite the same way as do other Jews—an impression buttressed by the controversy about their acceptability for purposes of marriage. Doubts about their acceptability as 'pure Jews' for purposes of marriage led the Sephardi Chief Rabbi in Israel to promulgate special directives in February 1962 requiring an investigation 'as far back as is possible' of the ancestry of Bene Israel contemplating marriage with members of other communities of Jews. The rabbis are of course required to check the status of any candidate for marriage, particularly one not born in Israel. But it is only as regards the Bene Israel that the rabbis were enjoined to inquire 'as far back as is possible' in a document that singled this community out in this particular respect.

True, in August 1964, the Chief Rabbinate Council agreed to delete the words 'Bene Israel' from the controversial directive— broadening the scope of the directive to apply to all Jews of whose status any suspicion or doubt arises. But while the original directive of 1962 received extensive publicity, the omission of the words 'Bene Israel' in the 1964 directive is rather less well known. In fact, many Jews seem ignorant of it. Moreover, even apart from the marriage controversy, there still exists a good deal of confusion about the status of the Bene Israel.

THE SETTING

At its peak, in the late 1940s, India's Jewish population numbered some 26,000. But owing to emigration—chiefly to Israel, and, to a lesser extent, to England—16,000 is much nearer the mark today. However, while the number of Jews in India is small, the divisions between them are many and deep.

Some 13,000 Jews are known as Bene Israel—Children of Israel. Bene Israel tradition maintains that they are descendants of members of the Ten Tribes of Israel who were shipwrecked off the west coast of India, not far from the present site of Bombay, in the second century B.C.E.[1] Only seven couples survived and their descendants were cut off from their co-religionists till recent times.

Nowadays about 10,000 Bene Israel live in the city of Bombay. Some 3,000 Bene Israel form small groups in various parts of the country. Until very recently Bene Israel were divided into two endogamous units, the Gora or White Bene Israel and the Kala or Black Bene Israel. Like Jews everywhere, Bene Israel have adopted some of the customs of the host society. Their mother tongue is Marathi, one of the main languages of western India; but very many of them also speak English.

The Jewish group on the south-west coast of India—reduced in numbers from 2,500 to 250 by emigration to Israel—is known as Cochin Jewry, although by no means all members of this group live in the town of Cochin. Cochin Jewry is divided into endogamous sub-groups: the Black Jews (formerly some 90 per cent of Cochin Jewry), the White Jews, and the Meshuararim. The last are the underprivileged descendants of the manumitted offspring of unions between Cochin Jews and their slave concubines; they are also divided into two groups, one of which is attached to the Black Jews and the other to the White Jews, according to descent. In comparison with the Black Jews, who resemble in physical features the people among whom they have been living for over a millennium, the White Jews, who are relatively fair-complexioned, are newcomers who migrated to India a few centuries ago. Nevertheless, the White Jews, claiming 'original and genuine' Jewish status, maintain that the Black Jews are merely the descendants of their converted slaves. Black and White Jews do not participate in one another's worship. Malayalam, the local language, is their mother tongue; but virtually all the White Jews (and some of the Black Jews) also speak English.

Some 2,000 Jews from Baghdad, with small additions from Aden, Afghanistan, and Iran, are known as Baghdadis. The first of the Baghdadis arrived in India over a century and a half ago. There is a Baghdadi community of some 900 in Bombay (formerly the Bombay Baghdadi community numbered over 2,000); there are also small groups of Baghdadis in Poona and Calcutta. Baghdadis are comparatively fair-complexioned. They consistently use English.

A few hundred European Jews, mainly from Germany and Austria, came to India in the 1930s. They live in Delhi, Calcutta, Madras, and especially in Bombay. Though the European Jews in Bombay often stress their differences from the Baghdadis, they join in Baghdadi social and religious activities.

Thus nearly three-quarters of Indian Jewry live in Bombay, a city of over four million people. As far as the west coast is concerned, Bombay—built on an island which is now joined to the mainland and so transformed into a peninsula—remains 'the Gateway of India', and from it radiate railways to every part of the country. The development of Bombay as a commercial city has attracted an extraordinarily polyglot population. Hindus—mainly Gujaratis and Maharashtrians—form the majority. But there are also large groups of Muslims and Indian Christians, and smaller groups of Jains, Sikhs, Parsis, Buddhists, and Europeans.

On the west side of the island are the select residential areas whose inhabitants live in beautiful houses surrounded by bright gardens or in modern apartments, built along tree-lined roads. On the east side are the docks. In the south, the Fort district, are the public buildings, offices, and large business premises. In the north end of the island is the industrial district, the mill area of Parel.

Midway between the Fort district and the mill area of Parel, not far from Bombay Central Station, lives the bulk of Bombay Jewry. It is a tenement area the majority of whose inhabitants— the poor of many communities—live in chronic want. Set in amidst the tenements are drab restaurants, from which come the strains of Indian music, and small shops; but many prefer to make their purchases in the bazaars where almost anything can be obtained quickly. The streets, whether long or short, are mostly narrow; during the day they are crowded and noisy, during the night they are transformed into a dormitory for the homeless. The poverty is all too obvious: but the sun, the colour, the crowds, the music, the vigorous turmoil of it all, seem to invest everything with courage and vitality and zest for life; I became enamoured of the neighbourhood—but I doubt whether this feeling was shared by many of its more permanent inhabitants.

FIELD WORK

This study is based on fifteen months' field work in Bombay and short stays among some of the small Bene Israel communities in other parts of India. Since very many of them also speak English, I hardly ever required an interpreter. In fact, a number of Bene Israel occasionally—and with much justice—commented upon my misuse of the English language. My attempts to learn Marathi provided both a source of amusement and proof of sincere interest in the community.

In Bombay I stayed in the University Settlement (administered by missionaries) which is within very close reach of the centre of the Jewish neighbourhood. Lodging with missionaries was not the drawback it might have been among some Jewish communities elsewhere. Bene Israel know of course that the chief aim of the missionaries is instruction in Christianity. But this, they relate, had an unsettling effect on only a few. On the other hand, the missionaries had much to offer—literacy in Marathi, the Bible in Marathi, instruction in Hebrew, introduction to English, 'greatly indebting our Bene Israel to them'. Indeed, I was sometimes under the impression that my lodging with the missionaries provided proof of my respectability.[2] But in any case, lodging with non-Bene Israel provided an advantage in that it prevented my becoming identified with a particular 'party' within the community.

In contrast to Western Jewries where a great deal of intellectual energy is taken up with the question of 'Who is a Jew?', Bene Israel content themselves with the statement that the community includes all those born into it and the few who have acquired membership not by birth but through conversion prior to marrying into the group. Even those who seem to have drifted away from Bene Israel society are looked upon as in some real sense still members of the community. I never heard of anyone being written-off as socially dead.

Obviously I cannot claim to have got to know all Bene Israel resident in Bombay—although I was frequently told, 'There cannot be many Bene Israel who haven't heard about you!' However, I did attend everything of a community nature that I could. The place in which I lived was not only within close reach of the communal neighbourhood but also very near to a synagogue which, because of a particularly energetic (some would say ambitious) committee, was one of the main centres of activities, involving not only its own members but the community as a whole. I spent so much time there that some came to refer to this synagogue as 'your office'. From the rolls of the synagogue I gathered much information. Committee members eagerly talked 'communal politics' and instructed me in the complexities of their undertakings. Congregants invited me to their homes, introduced me to their families and friends, sent invitations to their festivities, and so on. Cliques and clubs sent invitations to their meetings and outings.

The members of one of these clubs more or less adopted me, and I became a frequent visitor to their homes. From time to time their most active members would assemble to educate me and to give me information, one or two acting as spokesmen for the group. Moreover, Bene Israel whom I had met at communal functions would send me long letters about what the community thinks, says, and does. The quotations with which this book is studded are not a device to give immediacy to my account, but spring from these sources.

During my stay among the Bene Israel I met men and women of all ages and in a wide variety of situations. Many trusted me with intimate details of their lives and those of their families and friends. With a few I achieved a relationship of considerable friendship which still endures. Nevertheless, I was continually asked what I thought about the Jewishness of the Bene Israel— and I am not quite certain whether they believed me when I said that I never questioned the title of the Bene Israel to the full status of Jews.

In spite of the tension and even hostility between Bene Israel and their white co-religionists, my relations with Bene Israel were, I feel, happy ones. Very many Bene Israel held that a sincere study of their community would provide proof of the authenticity of their claim to belong to the House of Israel. Again, a number of Bene Israel about to go abroad asked for introductions to Jewish associations in England and Israel. Others hoped that I would be able to arouse the concern of Anglo-Jewry's charitable organizations in Bene Israel undertakings.

Moreover, that as a practising Jewess I worshipped with Bene Israel, rather than in the near-by synagogue of those claiming 'original and genuine' Jewish status, encouraged a feeling of familiarity, of 'oneness', which it might otherwise have been difficult to attain. On the other hand, the fact that Bene Israel do not *at first glance* conform to the image of Jews helped, I hope, to prevent my overlooking important features which familiarity might have obscured. The unexpected stimulates questions and guides research.

Because Bene Israel are comparatively few in number, it is exceedingly easy to identify informants and incidents, whatever the disguise; because of the interest which they take in everything that is written about them, it is not at all unlikely that some of them will chance upon this book; I have therefore thought it advisable to leave some statements unsupported by concrete examples. On the other hand, I have reserved the right to discuss the sociological significance of their historical memories, their caste-like characteristics, and their preoccupation with their status *vis-à-vis* other Jewish communities, regardless of some informants' fears that this might lower the Bene Israel in the eyes of their co-religionists. I do not believe that anything I have written could harm the Bene Israel. But in view of their sensitivity I feel it desirable to reaffirm my conviction of the validity of their title to the full status of Jews; indeed, I find any doubt on that matter distasteful.

NOTES

1. In giving dates I follow Jewish practice, using the initials B.C.E.— Before the Current Era—and C.E. It seems to me an amiable and proper practice to use the initials desired by those whom I describe.
2. It is of course true that Bene Israel need no longer rely on the missionaries for instruction in Hebrew. But most Bene Israel are conscious of and grateful for the help which the missionaries once rendered them.

2
The Lost Ten Tribes:
Bene Israel Historical Memories

The Bene Israel are known to have lived scattered in villages on the west coast of India, in the vicinity of the Island of Bombay, for a very long time. The question arises where this group—for centuries somewhat isolated from the general body of their co-religionists—came from, and how and when it came.

Of written records there are none: no important and authenticated references to the Bene Israel have yet been discovered in the annals and inscriptions of the neighbouring people, nor is there any special mention of them unearthed in early travellers' tales. Nevertheless, what people think of their past—whether or not it is dispassionate history—has relevance within the context of their social life.

THE LOST TEN TRIBES

Bene Israel maintain that they are descendants of members of the kingdom of the Ten Tribes of Israel. Such a claim has its counterpart in the tradition of the survival of the Ten Tribes and their eventual reintegration into the mainstream of Jewish life.

After the death of King Solomon in the tenth century B.C.E. only the tribes of Judah and Benjamin remained faithful to his son, forming the kingdom of Judah. Ten disaffected tribes seceded, establishing the kingdom of Israel. The latter kingdom came to an end with the fall of its capital, Samaria, in the second half of eighth century B.C.E. In accordance with Assyrian policy, part of the population—especially the nobility and the wealthier citizens—was deported. But while the people of the kingdom of Judah (deported by the Babylonians in the first half of the sixth century B.C.E.) retained their social identity, the deported Israelites seem to have vanished—hence one speaks of the 'Lost Tribes'.

The fate of the Ten Tribes of Israel is thus accounted for in 2 Kings 18:11, 'And the king of Assyria carried Israel away unto Assyria, and put them in Halah and in Habor, on the river of Gozan and in the cities of the Medes.' The deported Israelites—the fabled 'Lost Tribes'—ultimately lost their social identity; some were probably absorbed by the people among whom they were settled, while others became merged into those of their Judaean kinsmen with whom they came into contact.[1]

Yet many clung to the view that the deported Israelites had migrated from Assyria to different countries where they lived in their own communities in obscurity. During the Middle Ages credence was given to reports that the Ten Tribes had their own kingdoms and enjoyed great military power—reports which must have surprised and encouraged Jewish listeners subjected to many restrictions and persecutions. Indeed, it seems that the greater the persecutions to which Jewry was subjected, the more glamorous the life which the Ten Tribes of Israel were believed to enjoy.

The version which held the spellbound attention of the Jewish world and intrigued learned Christendom was put forward by Eldad Ha-Dani in the ninth century. Eldad claimed that he came from the home of four of the Ten Tribes of Israel. They had an independent state in East Africa beyond the Sambation river—a torrent carrying masses of sand and rubble with such terrific force that it would crush an iron mountain (but stilled on the Sabbath). His people, so Eldad continued, were brave warriors; they had multiplied exceedingly and enjoyed great wealth. When not busy with warfare, they occupied themselves with the study of the Bible.

This type of legend did not, however, satisfy succeeding generations, and the change in speculation as to the fate of the Ten Tribes is reflected in the following passage: 'In my childhood,' relates Benjamin II, the famous traveller who began his search for the Ten Tribes in 1844,

I had often heard of the ten tribes of Israel, who were said to have been banished to a dark and mountainous country, which was never comforted by the rays of the sun, or trodden by the foot of a stranger. It was said that they had their own government, and that under their own kings they rigidly adhered in these distant and unknown regions to the worship of Israel in the promised land. They were reputed to lead a marvellous life, whilst we, the descendants of the banished tribes of Judah and Benjamin, were obliged to languish in exile under the yoke of fanaticism. As I grew up, and devoted myself to the study of the Bible, I learnt from the Holy Writ that the other tribes of Israel had always been more corrupt than the tribes of Judah and Benjamin; and I said to myself: God is merciful and just, why does He permit those to be happy who least deserve it? From this moment I began to doubt the traditions of my people, especially as I could nowhere find in our holy books a satisfactory answer to this question, or obtain from them any explanations. The only alternative therefore was to travel and make my own observations; and this idea occupied me continually. When, in after years, this idea was acted on, I found the sought-for explanation and was led to the following conclusions: the fate which has befallen us, the children of Judah and Benjamin, is similar to that of the other tribes of Israel. Just as we have been driven out of one land, and have had to find a new refuge in another, so have the other ten tribes been compelled to wander from one country to another, to seek new places of shelter from their persecutions and sufferings.[2]

THE BENE ISRAEL STATEMENT OF
THE LOST TRIBES TRADITION

A claim to descent from members of the Ten Tribes deported by the Assyrians is not unusual.[3] Bene Israel, however, maintain that their ancestors belonged to the part of the population which had escaped deportation after the fall of the kingdom of Israel.[4]

In *The History of the Bene Israel of India*—many Bene Israel referred to it as 'the source-book of our history'—H. S. Kehimkar, a member of the Bene Israel community, writes:

It has been asserted by some that on the fall of the Kingdom of Israel, the ten tribes were entirely driven away by the Assyrian King from their country, but such was not the case; for according to 2 Chronicles 30, remnants were still here and there left in Palestine . . . their number was very much diminished owing to the frequent incursions that were made upon Palestine by foreign foes . . . Consequently there is every reason to suppose that many of the Hebrews of the ten tribes in the Northern Provinces would have left the country and sought refuge in obscure countries . . .[5]

Informants explained, 'Kehimkar, being a learned man, argued it all out. But he didn't invent anything! He merely wrote down our Bene Israel tradition.'[6]

Kehimkar argues:

Even so small a matter as a simple riot in Bombay which commenced on the 11th August 1893 and terminated on the 14th of that month between the Mahomedans and Hindus caused as many as 50,000 souls to desert Bombay for Gujarat and the Konkan; what innumerable multitudes, then, may have been induced to leave Palestine when that country was subjected to such frequent invasions for years together?

There seems reason to suppose that it was at the time of hostile inroads made into Palestine by foreign foes that the ancestors of the Bene Israel of the Bombay Presidency left their homes, and in particular about the time of the invasion of Antiochus Epiphanes. There were two routes ready for them at that time by which to travel to India.

Kehimkar adds:

. . . the tradition of the Bene Israel, handed down from father to son, corroborates the same view.[7]

But although they went to a new country, Bene Israel relate, 'they brought with them their old misfortunes'. For the ship in which the group travelled was wrecked off the Konkan, on the west coast of India not far from the present site of Bombay. Almost all the people were lost, with all their belongings, and only seven couples survived. The bodies of the drowned were washed ashore in the very village in which the survivors had taken refuge and buried there. The survivors had lost everything they had brought with them from their homes in the shipwreck and were in consequence reduced to a most miserable plight, 'more easily to be imagined than described'. The descendants of the seven couples were cut off from their co-religionists till recent times. As their numbers increased, they spread over the Konkan.

During their long isolation from their co-religionists, Bene Israel told me, they forgot Hebrew and a great part of Jewish ritual. This, Bene Israel argue, was only natural since they had lost the religious records they had brought with them in the shipwreck. However, they observed the Sabbath, some of the Holy-days, the dietary regulations, and circumcision; they remembered the *Shema*, the confession of the Jewish faith, and repeated it on every occasion, such as that of circumcision, marriage, and death. Moreover, Bene Israel relate that 'unions with alien women were frowned upon because the group wished to adhere to Jewish religious principles, and also because the Hindus, on account of their laws, were against marriage between Bene Israel and non-Bene Israel'. But Bene Israel acknowledge that while in ignorance of much of Jewish religion the group adopted some of the local customs—'foreign, it is true, to Judaism, but harmless and innocent, and not savouring in the slightest degree of an idolatrous tendency'.

INTERNAL EVIDENCE?

Bene Israel maintain that some of the ritual which they observed during their long isolation from their co-religionists was very similar to that practised in Israel in 175 B.C.E.—internal evidence for their migration from Israel at that time. Moreover, Bene Israel point out that the festival of Hanukkah and the four fasts of national mourning, which were not observed by them during their long isolation, had not been introduced in 175 B.C.E.[8]

It is not intended to argue here for or against the accuracy of Bene Israel historical memories. Nevertheless, it must be stated that the internal evidence adduced by the Bene Israel does not stand up to closer investigation. It may, of course, be possible to trace some similarity between the ritual observed by the Bene Israel during their long isolation from the mainstream of Jewish life and that practised in Israel in 175 B.C.E. However, the question arises whether there is not a much greater similarity between the ritual observed by the Bene Israel during their long isolation and that practised in India. In other words, one wonders whether the ritual observed by the Bene Israel during their long isolation was not copied from Hindu and Muslim examples rather than adapted from the ritual of Israel in 175 B.C.E.[9] Furthermore, non-observance of the festival of Hanukkah and the four fasts of national mourning cannot be accepted as evidence of the group's migration and isolation before their introduction, since Bene Israel did not observe some of the ritual which was certainly in use in 175 B.C.E.

Again, it must be stated that those who have interested themselves in the Bene Israel generally hold that this group came to
India from an Arabian country in the first millennium C.E. For
example, *The Gazetteer of the Bombay Presidency*[10] suggests that
the Bene Israel came to India from the Persian Gulf or Aden in
the sixth century C.E. In his *Appeal for the Christian Education of the Bene Israel*,[11] Wilson relinquishes his previous opinion
put forward in his *Lands of the Bible*[12] that the Bene Israel are
descendants of the Ten Tribes who had been settled in India for
many ages; instead he suggests that they came to India from the
Yemen in the middle of the first millennium C.E. And even Godbey,
who complains of the 'curious unwillingness to admit that
Israelites could have reached India in pre-Christian times'.
assumes that the Bene Israel came to India from an Arabian
country only sixteen centuries ago 'at a time when persecutions
begun by Sassanid Persians were driving thousands of Jews to
other lands'.[13]

However, Godbey argues, 'It is certain that any tradition of
descent from ancient Israel . . . may have originated in some
historic fact. This urges inquiry for the origin or meaning of . . .
such tradition. . . . It should be recognized that all such peoples
are the best judges' of whether they are descendants of the Ten
Tribes or not.[14] Still, Godbey admits, 'No other subject seems to
have had such fascination for the fanciful theorist. . . . Scores of
missionaries in various lands announced hasty conclusions. . . .
The "lost tribes" hunter has often been a Jew himself . . ."[15] It is
indeed possible that Bene Israel tradition of descent from the Ten
Tribes originated with Christian missionaries or Jewish travellers
who encountered them and from whom the group adopted it.
Finally, one wonders whether the Bene Israel, until they became
better acquainted with the Bible, were aware of the Lost Ten
Tribes tradition.

SIGNIFICANCE OF THE BENE ISRAEL TRADITION

Whether or not the tradition of the Bene Israel is based on some
'historic fact', cherished as it is in Bene Israel memory, it has
functional significance: for the tradition helps to define the posi-

tion of the Bene Israel in India, *vis-à-vis* the other Jewish community in western India, the Baghdadis, and *vis-à-vis* the generality of their co-religionists.

(a) In India

B. J. Israel, a member of the community, in an essay privately published, writes:[16]

> The legend that their ancestors were the survivors of a shipwreck at the village of Nowgaon near the port of Cheul may be based on truth. On the other hand, it may have been adopted when our people came to learn that, according to the Hindu Puranas, fourteen corpses of foreigners from a shipwreck on the Konkan coast were miraculously brought back to life by Parashuram, an *avatar* of the Hindu god Vishnu, and given the status of Brahmins. (The Chitpavan Brahmins of Maharashtra are supposed to be descended from these miraculously created Hindus.) The Puranic legend may have been appropriated by the Bene Israel with suitable modification to account for their presence on the coast.

But the tradition does somewhat more than merely account for the presence of the Bene Israel on the west coast of India. As Kehimkar suggests, '. . . the shipwreck encountered by the ancestors of the Bene Israel corresponds with the legend told of those of the Chitpavans on the same coast, and the identity of the alleged landing places of these tribes, these facts cannot but give rise in every thinking mind to the question: did the Bene Israel and the Chitpavans belong to the same stock?'[17]—and the Chitpavan Brahmins of Maharashtra, it must be remembered, are a highly placed, large and powerful caste.

(b) Vis-à-vis the Baghdadis

There are differences in colour, culture, occupation, wealth, etc. between the two Jewish groups in western India. Contrary to the egalitarianism enjoined by Jewish religion, Bene Israel complain, these differences are evaluated as higher and lower; and they cite examples, many of them perfectly credible, showing how badly their Baghdadi co-religionists have behaved towards them. Bene Israel say, 'These fair-complexioned Baghdadi Jews say that differences between our communities show that we are not "pure Hebrews". But we are!' And they argue that differences between the two communities merely testify to the truth of Bene Israel tradition. 'Differences are to be expected because we are descendants of the Ten Tribes. Does not our name prove it? Who else could we be?' Moreover, they complain about the view advanced by *The Gazetteer of the Bombay Presidency*—and others who have interested themselves in the community—to the effect that the Bene Israel came to India from an Arab country. 'If we came here from an Arab country would not the Baghdadis have more sympathy for us? Their attitude proves that we came here from Israel!'

(c) Vis-à-vis the generality of their co-religionists

But if the passionate insistence on descent from the Ten Tribes is related to the hostility between Bene Israel and Baghdadis— a response to the controversy in which Bene Israel have practically been challenged to prove the authenticity of their claim to belong to the House of Israel—it also provides a basis for the acceptance of Bene Israel by the generality of their co-religionists. It represents a charter for the relationship of Bene Israel to the rest of Jewry. For the claim to descent from members of the Ten Tribes of Israel, often put forward by Jewish communities which have been isolated for centuries from their co-religionists and influenced by a social system not usually associated with Judaism, correlates with the strong Jewish belief in the survival of the Ten Tribes and their eventual reintegration into the mainstream of Jewish life, and hence facilitates a renewal of social relations between these 'peripheral' Jewish communities and the general body of their co-religionists.

NOTES

1. Allen H. Godbey in *The Lost Tribes: A Myth*, Duke University Press, 1930, pp. 20, 684–5, considers the 'cavalier dismissal by some scholars' of claim upon claim to be survivors of ancient Israel 'most surprising'. Nevertheless, he writes, 'But we have no grounds' for using the term 'Jew' in contrast with 'ten tribes'. 'The deportees of the ten tribes are in all fairness to be viewed like deportees of the south,' the kingdom of Judah, 'simply as Jews of the Dispersion. . . .'
2. I. J. Benjamin, *Eight Years in Asia and Africa*, Hanover, 1863, pp.

266–7. (During his travels in India, towards the end of the eighteen-forties, Benjamin II encountered the Bene Israel; and indeed, he took the view that they are part of the descendants of the Ten Tribes of Israel.)

3. Non-Jewish groups, too, have claimed descent from the Ten Tribes of Israel. For example, Boyd S. Shafer in his *Nationalism: Myth and Reality*, London, 1955, p. 20, writes, 'In England in the nineteenth century an Anglo-Israel Identity Society went so far as to declare that the English people were descended from the Lost Tribes.' Certain Afghan tribes claim Israelite descent. Again, Godbey, ibid. pp. 1, 2, 5, relates, 'Some held that the Abyssinians were the "lost ten tribes". Others pressing further south, have found the "lost ten tribes" in the warrior-Masai. . . . The Israelitish origin of the Japanese has been infallibly demonstrated, and the same pedigree for the Malay is equally indisputable. . . .'

4. As has already been stated, only part of the population of the kingdom of Israel—the more influential element—was deported. (According to the Assyrian conqueror—surely the most likely to exaggerate the humiliations inflicted upon the conquered—the fall of Samaria after a three years' siege involved the deportation of 27,290 people; though no doubt there was more than one deportation. But the bulk of the people of Israel, those who had been too feeble to offer resistance and others who had been friendly to the Assyrians, remained behind.)

5. H. S. Kehimkar, *The History of the Bene Israel of India*, Tel-Aviv, 1937, pp. 6, 9, 10. The book was completed in 1897 and published some decades after the author's death by the good offices of Dr Immanuel Olsvanger of Jerusalem. (Whenever I asked my informants for the source of their historical memories, they replied, 'It's in Kehimkar's book.')

6. However, unlike most Bene Israel who maintain that their name—Children of Israel—suggests their descent from the Ten Tribes of Israel, Kehimkar argues that the name was adopted in order to avoid grating on Muslim sensibilities; ibid. pp. 74–5:

> . . . the name 'Bene Israel' was adopted by their ancestors during the time when the Mohamedan power prevailed in India, and Islam was propagated by the sword. The hatred which the Mohamedans bear towards the name Yehudi (Jew) as may be seen from the Koran, is in itself a ground for believing that our ancestors, through fear of being compelled to renounce their religion, or of losing their lives and property, thought it expedient to adopt the name less hated by the followers of Mahomed, viz. 'Bene Israel' (Children of Israel). . . . One fact may here be prominently brought forward in corroboration of the above statement.
>
> During the reign of Tippoo Sultan and the prosperity of the East India Company, that is, during the Second Mysore War (1780–84), several Bene Israel, who had enlisted in the service of the Honourable Company, were taken captives by Tippoo's army, and would have been put to the sword had they declared themselves 'Yahudim'. They were released in consequence of Tippoo's mother having begged of her son to spare the lives of the 'Bene Israel' so much talked of in the Koran, and whom she had never had the opportunity of seeing in India. In course of time their descendants made it a point to deny that they were 'Yahudim' or Jews. . . .

Bene Israel are of course familiar with the report of the encounter of these members of the community with the mother of Tippoo Sultan. But it is a tale told not in order to account for the adoption of the name 'Bene Israel', but in connection with the building of their first synagogue in 1796—the first in western India—built by one of them in gratitude for their escape from Tippoo Sultan. (There are indeed a number of small, isolated communities called 'Bene Israel' in Muslim countries. I do not know whether these small groups claim to have adopted the name to suggest descent from the Ten Tribes of Israel or to avoid persecution.)

7. Kehimkar, ibid. pp. 10, 12. I came across only two members of the Bene Israel community who were willing to concede that the community's tradition of descent from the Ten Tribes would not stand the test of a searching inquiry. These two were university graduates—but by no means the only university graduates with whom I discussed the subject. (Thus Shellim Samuel, a member of the community who is an advocate of the Supreme Court of India and a former professor of economics and politics, in his *Treatise on the Origin and Early History of the Beni-Israel of Maharashtra State*, Bombay, 1963, not only maintains that the Bene Israel are descendants of members of the Ten Tribes who came to India direct from Israel, but antedates the departure of the community from the Holy Land by over half a millennium. He writes that his ancestors, who apparently belonged to the tribes of Asher and Zebulun and were consequently in a position to control the sea-routes from Elath, had the foresight to recognize the hopelessness of their political plight about a decade before the fall of Samaria (in the eighth century B.C.E.) and set sail for Ophir in India. Nor, the author argues, is this at all surprising: for was not Ophir the main source of ancient Israel's wealth, and where could Ophir have been but in India?)

8. Godbey, ibid. p. 339, too, says that lack of knowledge of the festival of Hanukkah and the destruction of the Temple by the Romans (which led to the re-introduction of the four fasts of national mourning) 'seems decisive evidence of settlement in India long ere the Christian era . . .'. (I refer to this point again in note 13.)

9. Against this Kehimkar, ibid. p. 30, argues, 'Because some practice of making offerings had existed among gentile nations when a similar custom came into force among the Hebrews by Divine Command, could the conclusion at once be drawn that Moses had adopted the practice of making offerings from the Gentiles?'

10. *Gazetteer of the Bombay Presidency*, Bombay, 1885, vol. xviii, part 1, p. 506.

11. John Wilson, *Appeal for the Christian Education of the Bene Israel*, Bombay, 1866.

12. John Wilson, *Lands of the Bible*, Bombay, 1847, vol. 2, pp. 667–79.

13. Godbey, ibid. pp. 317, 345. This would seem to contradict Godbey's statement, quoted in note 8 above, that lack of knowledge of the festival of Hanukkah and the four fasts of national mourning seems decisive evidence of settlement in India long before the Christian era. However, Godbey assumes that the Bene Israel community does not owe its origin to one immigration. He may well be right. But he is wrong in stating that there are several traditions of immigration current among the Bene Israel. For although there may have been several immigrations, the group has long since fused into one community with but one tradition of

C

immigration—namely that the ancestors of the Bene Israel came to India two thousand years ago.

14. Godbey, ibid. p. 33.
15. Godbey, ibid. p. 2.
16. B. J. Israel, *Religious Evolution among the Bene Israel of India Since 1750*, Bombay, 1963, p. 4.
17. Kehimkar, ibid. p. 15.

3

The Dilemma of Caste

Whatever date one adopts for the arrival of the Bene Israel in India, the group has been part and parcel of life in the Konkan for centuries.[1] Not surprisingly, then, the group partakes to a certain extent of caste traditions.

Caste membership is acquired at birth, determines marriage, prescribes ritual, and is associated with a traditional occupation; and it is the duty of each individual to observe the laws of his caste. The castes are conceived of as existing in different degrees of spiritual dignity, the inegalities of the caste system being justified by the doctrine of rebirth. Under the doctrine a man's condition in this life is the result of his conduct in his last life: his high or low caste is therefore the reward or punishment of his past behaviour. The supreme object of the Brahman is to break the long cycle of rebirth and attain union with the divine soul.

Castes of high degree, barred from hundreds of lowly tasks which are yet necessary for their existence, need the services of those of low degree, while those of low degree need the ministrations of those of high degree for their spiritual salvation. Contact between those of different degrees of spiritual dignity produces pollution in those of high degree; hence the castes must be kept apart. Above all, castes are kept apart by the ban on intermarriage and the restrictions on commensality. The Hindu system, then, implies a mystically sanctioned, preordained interdependence and at the same time it stresses the social separation of caste from caste.

Caste also provides the pattern for relations with non-Hindu groups. Srinivas writes, 'Christians and Muslims were regarded as castes, too, and they accepted such a status. Even revolutionary movements which had aimed at the overthrow of the caste system ended by either becoming castes themselves or reproducing the caste system within themselves. The main body of Hindus regarded these sects as castes and not as sects.'[2] Again, Hutton says, 'Jews and Christians also in India often form castes . . . the caste system has afforded a place in society into which any community, be it racial, social, occupational or religious, can be fitted as a co-operating part of the social whole, while retaining its own distinctive character and its separate individual life.'[3]

Similarly, Mayer speaks of Muslim castes, adding, in a footnote, 'I use the word "caste" here advisedly'.[4] And Bailey writes that although Christian and Kond are not Hindu categories, 'as social groups within the village, they are in effect caste-groups'.[5]

Thus, while the position of the Bene Israel within Konkan society was not of the mystic and preordained kind bound up with the religious conceptions of Hinduism, Bene Israel were in many ways analogous to a caste. Indeed, Bene Israel tend to refer to themselves, and are referred to by their Indian neighbours, as a caste.

Bene Israel tradition has it that their ancestors took to oil pressing soon after their arrival in India.[6] Indeed, they were called 'Shanwar Teli'—Saturday oil-presser caste; 'meaning', Bene Israel relate, 'a caste of oil-pressers who did not work on Saturday'.[7]

One wonders whether Bene Israel were the oil-pressers *par excellence* in this area. For Mr S. V. Avalaskar, the Konkan historian, in a personal communication, writes, 'Practically every village (especially the bigger ones) had one or two families of the Bene Israel. . . . The Bene Israel abstained from the work of oil pressing on Saturdays, and the Konkan village community did not buy oil on Saturdays. This custom is being observed even today. The social restrictions not to buy oil on the day when the Bene Israel did not press oil appears to me very significant. . . .'[8]

It seems that Bene Israel stood low in the hierarchy of Konkan society. Indeed, a member of the Bene Israel community who had spent his youth in a Konkan village told me, 'We Bene Israel get on well with the Hindus. Hindus are gentle people and kind, and they do not like strife. Yet twenty years ago the Hindus in the Konkan still thought that if Bene Israel touched the utensils which Hindus used for food the utensils became polluted. The Hindus thought of us as Teli caste, and oil pressing is very humble work.' He added, 'But this has changed now—there has been much educational and also some economic improvement among the Bene Israel left in the Konkan. It has increased the respect in which Bene Israel are held—besides Hindus are less orthodox now.'[9]

But Kehimkar—whose main aim, it must be remembered, was to establish that the Bene Israel always regarded themselves, and were regarded by their Indian neighbours, as members of the Jewish religious group: and that Jewry must therefore accord them 'pure' Jewish status[10]—suggests that the low status of the Bene Israel in Konkan society was not the result of their being associated with a humble calling but due to their membership of a non-Hindu group. '. . . Hindus regarded it a pollution to touch a Mleccha or a man of a different religion; and the Bene Israel of course were included in the class of Mleccha.'[11] Kehimkar may well be right—although on another page he states, 'The natives of the Konkan, however, only took them for another of the several classes of oilmen already existing. . . .'[12]

In any case, apart from the extremities of the caste system, which were fixed, there is a certain vagueness regarding status in the hierarchy. True, Hutton writes that the pressing of oil seeds 'is stigmatized in the Code of Manu because it destroys life by crushing the seed'. In Bengal 'This seems to have led to the division of the caste into two'—one only dealing in oil while the other presses it—'one of which is treated as untouchable, the other not, and the Telis who only sell oil will outcaste a member who should venture to press it.'[13] On the other hand, Mayer relates that in Ramkheri, in Madhya Pradesh, the oil-pressers form part of the middle reaches of the hierarchy.[14] Moreover, there are variations in the status of non-Hindu groups. Hutton reports that generally speaking 'Muslims and Christians are regarded as inferior to Brahmans and Nayars in Malabar, but as less polluting than the lower castes, but Thurston records how he touched the ladle in a pot in which an Odh woman was cooking her meal and later found that she had been outcasted for subsequently touching the cooking pot.'[15] Again, Srinivas in his 'The Social System of a Mysore Village' acknowledges that there are 'excessive uncertainties' about the hierarchical position of Muslims in Rampura.[16]

Still, Professor Ezekiel writes of the humiliation and irritation he felt at being called 'Teli':

. . . when we first arrived in Alibag, after the retirement of my father in 1905, we were shocked to be described as Teli, and my mother as Telin, the feminine of Teli. I knew for certain that not for three generations had we known anyone in our family who had done the Oil-man's trade. Even in the John Elphinstone High School, most boys took delight in calling us by that very irritating name 'Teli'. I found to my surprise that some boys in the School had Ghanis or Oil-presses in their houses and their main source of income was the Oil-press. They were real Teli, but we always protested that we were not, not for some generations back. It may be there were some very far behind, we did not know. . . . We felt it very humiliating to be designated Teli. . . . We have risen far above that level and are now Doctors, Professors and even Principals of University Institutions.[17]

As Professor Ezekiel's indignation at being called 'Teli' decades after having abandoned this occupation indicates, it is never easy for a caste to raise its status in society—and may indeed take generations to achieve. But it certainly can be and has been done: by adopting some of the beliefs and practices of the higher castes —especially with regard to occupation, diet and marriage—a caste may sometimes succeed in increasing the estimation in which it is held.

Thus some Bene Israel succeeded in giving up oil pressing for more prestigeful occupations: they took to agriculture, in any case an occupation not restricted to particular castes. (Since no single village or group of neighbouring villages can support an indefinite number of specialists, the excess may abandon their traditional calling for agriculture or migrate to a near-by town.) Bene Israel also entered the army and fleet of the local rulers, rising to high positions, such as *Naik* (Commander) of the fleet of Angria, etc. Exceptional services were rewarded by land grants;[18] in addition such services were rewarded by edicts bestowing rights to special honour.[19]

Again, like Hindu castes wishing to rise in public esteem, Bene Israel adopted some of the canons of behaviour of the higher castes with regard to diet and marriage. Thus they refrained from eating beef and frowned at the re-marriage of widows.

'. . . the Hindu culture had sunk so deep into their bones,' Ezekiel writes, 'that in fact until very recently they believed that beef was prohibited to them in the Old Testament.'[20] A member of the Bene Israel community told me, 'I am an orthodox man, though I must admit that I have eaten beef once or twice.' A few Bene Israel asked me, 'Do the Orthodox Jews in England eat beef?' (Virtually all Bene Israel now know that beef eating is not prohibited in the Old Testament.)

However, Kehimkar suggests that prudence rather than past ignorance of Jewish dietary rules prompted the Bene Israel to abstain from eating beef.[21] 'We need not go far to seek for a proof. . . . At Alibag in December 1884, it was alleged that certain Bene Israel had slaughtered a cow, and the whole Bene Israel community had to make satisfaction for the crime. The matter was brought to the notice of Angria's widow who had at once by her influence had a stop put to the Bazaar supplies of the Bene Israel; consequently they had to obtain them from other stations, and this state of affairs continued for a fortnight, when the Bene Israel proved that the charge was a false one, and passed a written document to the following effect:

> We, the Bene Israel of Alibag, bind ourselves by an agreement to the Hindu inhabitants of Alibag. Owing to the general out-cry against the Bene Israel of having committed a deed (of slaughtering a cow) against the Hindu religion, you have prohibited the holding of any intercourse with us. But having been assured by us of our not being connected with the deed, you have freed us from the imposition. We thank you for that. No such deed was up to this date perpetrated at Alibag. In like manner, neither we nor our descendants will ever perpetrate a deed of the above kind against the Hindu religion. If we should directly or indirectly act, or encourage others to act, against this writing, you are free to hold no more intercourse with us, and we make no objection to any arrangement you may make. This agreement was made on our free will, while in sound mind and not otherwise. 23rd December 1884.

Thus they were freed from the imposition.

Again, Bene Israel said, 'Is it necessary for a widow to re-marry? Of course, if she has many children and has not been provided for financially—then she may not be able to avoid it. What to do? But even then it is not very nice for a widow to re-marry.' A young woman of the Bene Israel community told me that her mother had been widowed very soon after marriage. Nevertheless, her mother's father asked his widowed daughter not to consider re-marriage. 'Nowadays there are some people in our community who do not worry about widow re-marriage. But we are one of the best families in our community, so my grandfather could not want his widowed daughter to re-marry.' The grandfather of this informant confirmed that he had persuaded his widowed daughter not to re-marry. 'You may think of our practice as assimilation to the Hindu system. But we know that widow re-marriage is not prohibited in the Bible! And we Bene Israel do not prohibit widow re-marriage, we merely frown upon it. But don't you think that the Hindu attitude to widow re-marriage goes one better than the Bible? So Bene Israel attitude to widow re-marriage goes one better than the Bible! And it not this a good thing?'

But it seems that the attempts of the Bene Israel to raise their status in the Konkan hierarchy met with limited success. Nor is this surprising: change in caste status requires not only change of custom *within* the caste but also change in the activities *between* the castes. This is in line with Mayer's sensitive distinction between overt and covert efforts to improve rank. 'The former consists in making demands, or in taking action which clearly shows one's pretensions. . . . Covert policies are those which improve the caste's prestige, in the hope that sooner or later it will be recognized as having risen.'[22] The terms 'interaction' and 'attributional' have been used by McKim Marriott to distinguish changes in the activities between castes from mere adoption of the canons of behaviour of the higher castes.[23] Again, Dumont and Pocock emphasize that mere imitation 'without some other economic or political factor brings about no change in the relative position of castes'.[24] (Indeed, apprehension that change of caste custom requires strenuous efforts, involving economic and emotional hardship, in return for small rewards may help to account for the comparative slowness in the adoption of the practices of the higher castes.)

It is not suggested here that Bene Israel, whose position in Konkan society was not of the mystic and preordained kind bound up with the religious conceptions of Hinduism, formed a caste proper. Nevertheless, it has been shown that features belonging to a caste structure entered into the relations between Bene Israel and Hindus: like other groups, Bene Israel were associated with a traditional occupation; relations between Bene Israel and Hindus were governed by the concept of pollution;

oriented in terms of the caste system, Bene Israel adopted some of the practices and values of those privileged and endowed with a higher dignity and, like other lowly placed groups, thereby attempted to raise their position in Konkan society.[25] Indeed, even Kehimkar, who maintains that the Bene Israel 'kept themselves aloof' and did not adopt Hindu values, on occasion reveals an orientation to the caste system: members of the Bene Israel family of Ashtamkar 'resemble very much the Konkanasth Brahmins', he notes with great approval, and are 'well known for speaking pure Marathi . . . equally good as that used by Brahmins in the midst of whom they have been living for several generations'.[26]

Moreover, features belonging to a caste structure also entered into the relations of Bene Israel with one another. Bene Israel were divided into two units, the Gora or White Bene Israel and the Kala or Black Bene Israel. The former are believed to be the pure descendants of the seven couples who landed in the Konkan, the latter are known to be the offspring of unions between Bene Israel men and non-Bene Israel women—although it is obvious from the appearance of the Gora that some unions between their ancestors and non-Bene Israel must have taken place. Indeed, there are Gora, White Bene Israel, who are darker than Kala, Black Bene Israel.

Against this Gora Bene Israel maintain, 'It is not skin colour which tells us who is Kala. It is known in the community who is Kala. There are some Gora who are a little dark—but not because of mixed unions! Poverty and the excessive heat of India greatly affected the fair complexion of our ancestors.'

One informant argues that it 'depends on the skin colour of the original migrants, which may have been fair to dark, as among the Yemen Jews. Many Yemen Jews are as dark as the darkest Bene Israel. So we may have brought our colour with us. Colour is no index of admixture. My father always held that the "pure" Jew is dark. It is the white Jew who is mixed!'

However distorted this point of view—for it so happens that Jews everywhere resemble in physical features the people among whom they have been living for centuries; and it is somewhat difficult to believe that Jews with dark skins living in countries inhabited by people with dark skins brought their skin colour with them, while Jews with light skins acquired their skin colour through intermarriage—it is nevertheless significant: revealing with ferocious clarity, as it does, the social importance of differences in physical features between Jews. Fortunately there is no need to speculate about the skin colour of the ancient Jew: the Mishnah—the oldest collection, apart from the Pentateuch, of Jewish legislative writings, concluded about 200 C.E.—negaim, 2, 1, tells us that Jews 'are neither white nor black but of the intermediate shade'.

It would seem therefore that Kala are the offspring of mixed unions which for some reason or other have been remembered, while unions between the ancestors of the Gora and non-Bene Israel have been forgotten—perhaps the ancestors of the Kala contracted unions with non-Bene Israel later than did those of the Gora.

Kehimkar maintains that Kala are the offspring of 'illicit unions, either temporary or permanent', and not of intermarriages proper. He implies, moreover, that, although the very existence of Kala 'shows that the state of morality was once lower than it is now', illicit unions are less of an 'abomination' than intermarriages proper.[27] Similarly, Hutton relates, 'It is not uncommon in some parts of India for a man of one caste to keep a concubine of a lower caste, or even a non-Hindu, and he is not outcasted by his caste fellows on that ground. . . .' But '. . . a person marrying outside the caste is excommunicated.'[28]

Until some years ago, Gora and Kala neither intermarried nor interdined. A woman of the Bene Israel community told me, 'My mother used to get furious when Kala came near her cooking utensils, and would push them away. She would not allow Kala to touch any utensils which she used for food.' Gora and Kala worshipped in the same synagogue. But Kala were given the sanctified wine, distributed in the synagogue after the service on Sabbaths and Holy-days, only after Gora had been served. Moreover, Kala were not permitted to wear the *Tallith*—a ritual garment worn by Jews during the morning service in the synagogue.

It appears that Kala could not raise their status. Kehimkar relates that in 1846 a wealthy man who exercised great influence over the community

attempted to introduce his own child born from an alien woman as a real Bene Israel by taking that child to a public feast to dine from the same dish with him and others; the Bene Israel strongly objected to it. As soon as the child sat at the table, the whole party present on the occasion dispersed, being greatly indignant at this attempt to remove the anciently recognized distinction between the real Israel and Black or Kala Israel.[29]

In the second half of the nineteenth century Kala engaged in a strenuous struggle for ritual equality. 'The "Black" Israel of the present day try their utmost to eradicate this distinction,' Kehimkar relates, 'as will be seen by a reference to the correspondence published in a Marathi journal and from a pamphlet published in 1880 entitled "Reflections on the Caste Distinction among the Bene Israel" by a member of the Bene Israel community. . . . Similar attempts have also been made in times past by that class.... Large and handsome donations were promised to the synagogue in the event of the request being complied with.' But the request, Kehimkar writes, was refused—a refusal which 'rankled deeply' in Kala minds. Eventually, however, 'the injustice' of allowing invidious distinctions in the synagogue 'having been made clear to the community, it was discontinued'.[30]

As a result of the elaboration of economic, educational, and general social activities among the Bene Israel, divisions between those in prestigeful professions and the clerk element tend to replace the Gora and Kala groupings. Indeed, nowadays open reference to Kala descent is recognized as an unpardonable error in taste. Hence Kala are no longer drawn together by common interests, such as the need to take co-operative action. Gora assert, 'Nowadays only the most sensitive of them are Kala-conscious.'

But while Gora no longer discuss the subject openly, a Gora may point out a Kala behind his back—especially if he is on bad terms with him. In this manner I came across about fourteen Kala elementary families. Gora are not certain about the number of Kala, though they hold that there are more than fourteen Kala elementary families—in theory, Gora informants asserted, it would be possible to count Kala, but in practice it would be a troublesome and even shocking thing to do. But although there is no overt roll, I have never heard anyone being classed as Kala by one person and as Gora by another. Bene Israel insist, 'We know who's what.' Again, an informant told me, 'We are not hush-hush about the subject. Kala families are not many; they are openly recognized as such; and several Kala families make no attempt to conceal the fact. . . .'[31]

A Gora informant told me, 'Most people don't worry about Gora and Kala these days. After all, Gora and Kala observe the same religious practices. We are all equal! But when it comes to marriage, most Gora don't like their children to marry Kala. Yet there have been some marriages between Gora and Kala in recent years. What to do? But don't mention that I discussed the subject with you! Perhaps I should not have talked about it. Kala will be hurt. After all, now all are equal. I told you because you are interested in it from a sociological point of view. So it isn't gossip!'

Like Hindu castes, Gora and Kala were conceived of as existing in different degrees of spiritual dignity: Gora, believed to be of pure blood, were exalted, while Kala bore the stigma of their descent. Moreover, the restrictions on social relations between Gora and Kala resemble the restrictions on social relations between Hindu castes. Nevertheless, Gora and Kala cannot legitimately be considered to have formed a fully fledged caste system. Relations between them were not conceived of as preordained or even as necessary. There was no interdependence. Certainly Gora did not need the services of Kala. True, Kala worshipped in the synagogue of the Gora; but, had they desired it, Kala could have established their own place of worship—as the underprivileged Meshuararim once did in Cochin.[32] Gora and Kala come closest to the subcaste pattern: co-existing but not complementary to one another. Another feature which points to the subcaste-like relationship between Gora and Kala is that *vis-à-vis* Indian society they formed an undifferentiated group—for subcastes, as Mayer emphasizes, 'are generally equal in the eyes of outsiders. . . . On the whole, caste membership is significant for relations with other castes, and subcaste membership for activities within the caste.'[33]

Obviously, Bene Israel were in many ways assimilated to their environment. And while assimilation is a distasteful word in many Jewish circles, every Jewish community tends to exhibit a distinct local colouring. Not even the most intransigent of Jewish communities can be said to have escaped it altogether.

For example, I have referred to Bene Israel dislike of widow re-marriage as an example of assimilation to the Hindu system. But the ban on polygyny among Western Jewry represents an example of assimilation on lines similar to the dislike for widow re-marriage among the Bene Israel. (Western Jews, however, only claim that the ban on polygyny is in line with the values of Judaism, unlike Bene Israel who hold that the dislike for widow re-marriage 'goes one better than the Bible'.)

Again, I have related that Bene Israel tend to refer to themselves, and are referred to by their Indian neighbours, as a caste. But, then, the way a Jewish community sees itself, and is seen by others, issues to a large extent from the social system of the society within which it exists. (For example, in Canada the Jewish community is regarded and regards itself as a cultural unit, like the Anglo-Saxons and the French.)

Clearly, then, certain aspects of Bene Israel assimilation can readily be duplicated in other Jewish communities. The peculiarity of Indian Jewry's situation lies in the fact that it is assimilated to a system not usually associated with Judaism—unlike Islam and Christianity which have confronted Judaism for many centuries—a system which, moreover, sits uneasily on the followers of an egalitarian religion.

For caste represents a dilemma for Jews—indeed for anyone who believes in equality. It is true that the caste system made it possible for Indian Jews—as for other religious, racial, social or occupational groups—to blend into Indian society without losing their own distinctive character and their separate individual life. On the other hand, a hierarchy of ritual rank has no meaning in Judaism, and Jews might be expected to repudiate caste altogether. Not surprisingly, then, as long as the Bene Israel were somewhat isolated from the mainstream of Jewish life, they tended to accept a caste-like state of affairs; but once continuous contact with their co-religionists was established, the painful consequences of caste soon became apparent.

NOTES

1. Mr S. V. Avalaskar, the Konkan historian, who was kind enough to discuss the subject with me, said, 'It is not known when the Bene Israel first settled in the Konkan, though they must have been there for a number of centuries.'
2. M. N. Srinivas, *Religion and Society among the Coorgs of South India*, Oxford, 1952, p. 31.
3. J. H. Hutton, *Caste in India*, 2nd ed., London, 1951, pp. 2, 115.

4. Adrian C. Mayer, *Caste and Kinship in Central India*, London, 1960, p. 34.
5. F. G. Bailey, *Caste and the Economic Frontier*, Manchester, 1957, p. xv.
6. Professor M. Ezekiel, himself a member of the Bene Israel community, writes in his booklet, *History and Culture of the Bene Israel in India*, Bombay, 1948, p. 8, '. . . there was a rich oil merchant owning a number of country oil-presses. . . . It was he who took pity on these destitute people and gave them work. . . . It was thus that they learnt the oil-pressing business as their first profession and it appears that they carried it through for many generations.' However, Kehimkar, whose main aim is to provide proof that the Bene Israel are indeed 'pure Hebrews' who came to India direct from Israel, suggests, ibid. p. 37, 'Staple commodities of export from Palestine in ancient times were, we know, oil and agricultural products. . . .' Bene Israel took to oil pressing 'which they had probably followed in their own mother-country . . . incidentally a collateral argument in support of their true Israelitish descent'.
7. Some Bene Israel informants said to me, 'You must be wondering whether we were known as Bene Israel or as Saturday oil-pressers or as both. We think it was like this: Our ancestors wished to be known as Bene Israel. But our oil pressing so impressed the people in the Konkan that they preferred to call us "Shanwar Teli"—Saturday oil-presser caste. It took some time before they began to call us Bene Israel.' Kehimkar, ibid. p. 2, relates that it was under the British that the community succeeded in getting itself generally known by the name Bene Israel.
8. However, Professor G. S. Ghurye, who was good enough to discuss this point with me, suggested that if the Konkan village community abstained from oil buying on Saturdays, the abstention must be explained in terms of Konkan Hindu ritual and not in connection with the Bene Israel oil-pressers. (But is it not possible that in course of time Konkan Hindus also came to connect abstention from oil buying on Saturdays with the Bene Israel oil-pressers who rested on that day? At any rate, Mr Avalaskar seems to have done so.)
9. This informant said too, 'Perhaps I should not have told you this. Most Bene Israel would not have told you this. They don't want to remember. Perhaps they don't remember. . . .'
10. The controversy about the 'pure' Jewish status of the Bene Israel has already been referred to, and will be discussed in some detail in the following chapter.
11. Kehimkar, ibid. p. 56.
12. Kehimkar, ibid. p. 37.
13. Hutton, ibid. p. 89.
14. Mayer, ibid. p. 36.
15. Hutton, ibid. p. 82.
16. Srinivas, 'The Social System of a Mysore Village', in *Village India*, ed. Marriott, Chicago, 1955, p. 22.
17. Ezekiel, ibid. pp. 26–7. (Alibag is a Konkan township.)
18. A member of the Bene Israel community told me that the land he owned had been granted to his ancestors in recognition of exceptional services rendered to the local ruler. Moreover, he related that other Bene Israel, too, had been in possession of such land grants but had since sold them.

19. Kehimkar, ibid. pp. 80–1, quotes an edict issued by a Konkan ruler in in 1761 consequent upon a petition by Tanaji bin Succoji *Naik*:

> . . . the petitioner by descent through a line of ancestors served His Royal Highness from generation to generation with great devotion and loyalty, and trusts to do the same in future; that whereas the office of Naik which the predecessors of His Highness were graciously pleased to confer on his ancestors has also been held by the successive members of his family, and that on the occasion of weddings or festivities in the community certain honours and presents were accustomed to be rendered first to the Kaji, then to the members of his family and lastly to the people of the community, and that such was the practice in force hitherto is still evidenced by vestiges of it still remaining, such as the presents of betelnut and leaves which are still in vogue; and that he prays that His Highness might be pleased to allow the members of his family to enjoy these honours and privileges in full as in times heretofore. We therefore issue a Royal edict that after the Kaji has been served with honours and presents, the same shall be given to the Naik, and then be distributed to the members of the community; that when there is no person of the Naik's family present, then they shall be given to the Kaji, and afterwards to the community; and that no one shall object to this right being enjoyed by the said Naik's family. After the Kaji has received the honours and presents, they are to be given to the Naik, who shall from generation to generation enjoy the same, from father to son. . . .

Kehimkar adds, 'But it is to be observed that although the office of Naik was abolished from the time that Angria's fleet was burnt by the Peshwa, yet the descendants of Naik look back to it with pride and are offended if they are not designated as such.' (Kehimkar wrote at the end of the last century.) The *Kaji* office will be discussed in the following chapter.

20. Ezekiel, ibid. p. 64.
21. Kehimkar, ibid. p. 24.
22. Mayer, ibid. p. 48.
23. McKim Marriott, 'Interactional and Attributional Theories of Caste Ranking', *Man in India*, vol. 39, No. 2, 1959.
24. L. Dumont and D. Pocock, *Contributions to Indian Sociology*, No. 1, 1957, p. 35.
25. The Berreman-Dumont controversy in *Contributions to Indian Sociology*, No. 5, pp. 20–43, No. 6, pp. 11–15, raises the problem whether caste refers exclusively to the system peculiar to Hindu India or can be applied to any kind of structure of exceptional rigidity. But in talking of the caste-like features of Bene Israel relations I am not entering into the vexed question whether caste is a matter of structure which has world-wide application. For Bene Israel, though not a Hindu category, are part of the Indian world of whose traditions they partake.
26. Kehimkar, ibid. pp. 56, 61, 90.
27. Kehimkar, ibid. p. 51. Recently, however, some marriages proper between Bene Israel and non-Bene Israel have taken place. Nowadays such unions tend to be preceded by the woman's conversion to Judaism. (Many of my informants appeared uncertain whether or not the offspring of such unions are Kala.) Intermarriage will be discussed in some detail in a later chapter.
28. Hutton, ibid. pp. 71, 63–4.

29. Kehimkar, ibid. p. 32. Kehimkar was born in 1830 and it is possible that he witnessed this incident. (The phrase 'a real Bene Israel'—that is, a real Children of Israel—is of course grammatically incorrect; it is most unusual for Kehimkar to use Hebrew incorrectly.)

30. Kehimkar, ibid. pp. 31–2, 33. The correspondence referred to appeared in the Marathi journal *Satya Prakasha* (The Light of Truth), vol. 2, pp. 29–36, 87–88, published by the Bene Israel in 1878–9. (Again, the man mainly responsible for the failure of the attempt to eradicate distinctions between Gora and Kala in return for a handsome donation was the father of the person whose child 'born from an alien woman' was refused permission to dine from the same dish with 'real Bene Israel'.)

31. Nevertheless, in a recent communication this informant writes, 'The prejudice still survives.' And he relates the case of a member of the community in a prestigeful occupation who jilted a well-educated Kala girl on learning of her origin—although he had taken the initiative and sent an offer to the girl's parents who presumed that he was aware of their Kala origin. However, I gather that the man had been away from Bombay for a long time, which may account for his ignorance of the girl's Kala origin. On the other hand, it is possible that the girl's Kala descent was merely an excuse to break the engagement. (Similarly, Mayer, ibid. p. 219, relates the case of a man who sent his wife away because she had insulted his mother. Some people agreed that this was right: 'the son should put his mother before anyone else'. Still, Mayer adds, 'One might question whether there were not other underlying reasons for the man's action, and certainly there are enough instances of men leaving a household because their wives had quarrelled with their mothers to show that a man does not always stick by his mother.')

32. S. S. Koder in his 'The Jews in Malabar', *India and Israel*, Bombay, May 1951, relates, 'About a hundred years ago, the Meshuararim, unable to bear the insults of the White Jews any longer, revolted and shifted *en masse* from Jew Town to British Cochin where they built a prayer hall and a cemetery.' (Jew Town is the name of the long narrow street granted by the Raja of Cochin some centuries ago.) Cochin Jews relate that a plague diminished the numbers of the Meshuararim, obliging them to return to Jew Town; but both the prayer hall and the cemetery are still in existence.

33. Mayer, ibid. pp. 159 ff. (It was only in the 1880s, when doubts concerning the 'purity of the blood of the Bene Israel' were raised, that Gora tried to impress upon outsiders that Bene Israel did not form an undifferentiated group but were rigidly divided according to purity of descent.)

4

Leaders and Teachers

An informant writes, 'The advent of David Rahabi is a memorable event in the history of the Bene Israel, not, as generally supposed, for bringing back to them the religion of their forefathers, for that the Bene Israel had never lost, but for breaking that barrier of isolation which for long centuries had prevented all communication with Jews in other parts of the world.'

According to Bene Israel tradition David Rahabi is supposed to have stumbled upon the community by accident. Bene Israel are uncertain about the date of Rahabi's coming; some hold that he came about a thousand years ago, others say that he came some five hundred years ago; and so forth. Because the word 'Rahab' is occasionally used in the Bible to designate Egypt,[1] many Bene Israel deduce that Rahabi came from that country, and, moreover, that Rahabi was none other than the brother of Moses Maimonides, one of Jewry's greatest figures.

B. J. Israel argues:[2]

Some people believe that the legendary teacher was a brother of Moses Maimonides named David who, according to a letter of Moses Maimonides written in 1176 C.E., was drowned while travelling in the Indian Ocean. Now this brother, who was a trader, is not known to have visited that part of India in which the Bene Israel were to be found. Nor is there any ground to presume that he ever encountered the Bene Israel, still less that he stayed among them and taught them as the legend relates. This belief is not based on any old Bene Israel tradition. It appears to have stemmed from a reference to the Jews of India in another letter of Moses Maimonides written to the Rabbis of Lunel in 1199 or 1200 C.E., which became known to the Bene Israel only after 1900.

D

But whether or not the belief that Rahabi was the brother of Moses Maimonides is based on an old communal tradition, it is widely held. Indeed, some Bene Israel were exceedingly angry with me for doubting it! (One cannot help suspecting that the determination to identify Rahabi with the brother of Moses Maimonides is related to the tension which exists between the Bene Israel and their co-religionists: if the brother of the great Maimonides was convinced that Bene Israel form part of the House of Israel, what right has anyone to question it?)

Olsvanger, who published Kehimkar's book in 1937, comments, 'What documents or references are there to prove the historicity of this David Rahabi?'[3] However, there is a document to prove the real existence of this man. For there is a Rahabi family in Cochin in whose unpublished family history, written in Hebrew, I have read that a member of the family, David Ezekiel Rahabi, went to western India in the middle of the eighteenth century, in the course of his work for the Dutch East India Company, there encountered the Bene Israel, and revived the Judaism he found existent among them. Indeed, Kehimkar relates that a family with the surname Rahabi is found in Cochin.[4] Nevertheless, he maintains that Rahabi did not come from Cochin. For such an admission would lead one to ask whether David Rahabi was really the first Cochin Jew to come across the Bene Israel and would thus undermine the Bene Israel tradition that their isolation from their co-religionists until recent times—an isolation which, Bene Israel assert, accounts for their past orientation to the Hindu social system—was interrupted but once. And even the few Bene Israel who told me that they were inclined to doubt the accuracy of the group's historical memories and, who, moreover, hold that Rahabi came from Cochin in the middle of the eighteenth century, nevertheless maintain that Rahabi was the only Cochin Jew to stumble upon the Bene Israel prior to the nineteenth century.

Kehimkar relates:[5]

> Although David Rahabi was convinced that the Bene Israel were the real descendants of the Hebrews, he still wanted to test them further. He therefore, it is said, gave their women clean and unclean fish to be cooked together; but they promptly singled out the clean fish from the unclean ones, saying that they never used fish that had neither fins nor scales.

It seems a credible tale. In Judaism what one may or may not eat is meticulously defined; it is almost impossible for an Orthodox Jew to enjoy a normal diet when travelling unless he encounters Orthodox co-religionists during his travels. Rahabi, encountering the Bene Israel, naturally tried to ascertain whether they observed the rules relating to food. (Indeed, that Rahabi is reported to have tested Bene Israel observance of the rules relating to fish seems to me to add credence to the tale: it is extremely difficult to test observance of the rules relating to meat—which would require the knowledge of the technique of ritual slaughter—but comparatively easy to establish whether the rules relating to fish are observed.)

Being thus satisfied, Rahabi began to teach the Bene Israel the tenets of the Jewish religion.

THE KAJI OFFICE

Bene Israel tradition says that Rahabi taught them Hebrew, organized their prayers, introduced them to early and late outgrowths of the religion of their forefathers, and appointed three *Kajis*[6] from among those he had taught—young men from the Jhiratkar, Shapurkar and Rajpurkar families—to be teachers and preachers in the community.

As Bene Israel were dispersed over scores of villages, the *Kajis* travelled wherever required to settle disputes and attend important ceremonies like circumcision and marriage. The *Kaji* office was hereditary. Moreover, *Kaji* hereditary privileges were confirmed by the local rulers who granted them *Sanads*—warrants conveying authority.

Kehimkar cites some of these *Sanads*; the following *Sanad*, granted in 1840, a renewal of a *Sanad* issued in 1770, provides an inkling of the *Kaji's* position and activities:[7]

A Sanad granted by the Valiant King . . . Jacob Eloji and his brothers Saturday oilmen inhabitants of the village Khursai in the district of Mhuslay came in person and handed in a petition to the effect that their hereditary rights as Kajis had been withheld from them for three years although they were in possession of a Sanad granted in the name of their ancestors. . . . This Sanad . . . has become very old, they have requested me to renew the same and to restore them their rights as Kajis. Having duly considered their Petition, His Majesty has come to this decision: that the Shanwar Telis herein before-named are legally entitled to enjoy the inheritance of the rights and privileges as Kajis . . . and has renewed the Sanad duly sealed. It is hereby proclaimed that all marriage ceremonies, domestic convivialities and funeral rites should be conducted and performed by Kajis agreeably to former rules, and that any caste dispute should be settled by them. It is also proclaimed that the Kajis should be duly honoured and respected as before . . . and that whenever they build a house they should be provided with gratuitous labour. . . . Further they should not be obliged to have their Sanad renewed every year. . . . The hereditary rights of the Kajis should on no account be interfered with and should be continued from father to son and from generation to generation. . . .

Thus it seems that already in the 1830s the *Kajis* had to struggle for their privileges. Kehimkar, writing at the end of the 1890s, adds,[8] 'The Kajis have now ceased to hold any authority in the community, on account of their ignorance in matters religious and secular, and of their want of zeal in maintaining the Hebrew religion among their flock.' (Ignorance in matters secular is probably a greater drawback than ignorance in matters religious. For, as will be shown in later chapters, Bene Israel tend to evaluate secular knowledge and achievements as higher than religious knowledge, and it would nowadays be exceedingly difficult for anyone to gain esteem in the community on the basis of religious knowledge only.) But although the *Kajis* no longer hold any authority in the community, some of their descendants look back upon the office with great pride; moreover, a few still like to describe themselves as *Kajis*. Indeed, I noticed that in the 1959 report of the Bene Israel school one subscriber added the title to his name. I have also seen the title engraved on fairly recent gravestones in the Bene Israel cemetery in Bombay.

But did Rahabi introduce the *Kaji* office? It appears that the *Kajis* were established and in possession of *Sanads* before the middle of the eighteenth century.[9] Hence it follows that the *Kaji* office was in existence before the arrival of David Rahabi. It is likely that Rahabi chose for training those who already held authority in the community, and that this training lent further prestige to the *Kaji* office. In any case, the term *Kaji* has not been in use in other Jewish communities; and it is reasonable to presume that, had Rahabi been the initiator of the office, he would have transferred to it the name by which it was known in his own environment. Some Bene Israel with whom I discussed this point argued, 'They may have adopted a Muslim term to show good will towards their Muslim neighbours with whom they came into contact. But this does not suggest that Rahabi did not introduce the *Kaji* office.' Some added, 'Muslims are monotheists. So there is no shame in using their term for the religious leader of our Bene Israel community.'

THE MOVE TO BOMBAY

Some time during the eighteenth century Bene Israel began to move to Bombay. Gravestones excavated in an old Bene Israel cemetery in Bombay indicate that a small group must have been resident there in 1776. Again, a document in the handwriting of one Samuel Nissim Kaji dated 1800 states that Bene Israel first settled in Bombay in 1746. In 1833 some 2,000 Bene Israel, that is, a third of the group, lived in Bombay. They were drawn beyond the narrow original limits of their Konkan home by the demand for skilled labour, such as carpentry, which was created by the expansion of the town, and by the chance of military service. Many enlisted in the regiments of the East India Company, rising rapidly to positions of responsibility.[10] Bene Israel say, 'Much employment and education could be found in Bombay, offering our people greater responsibility and social advancement. . . . In Bombay Bene Israel became a clerk caste.' One of my informants remarked, 'All this may not sound very much to you—but when one considers that we started as an oil-presser caste, without push or influence, we need not feel ashamed!'

The move to Bombay led to more than mere change of habitat and occupation. In the Konkan Bene Israel had been dispersed over many villages, forming part and parcel of the life in the village in which they found themselves. Spatial proximity and many common cultural forms made the Bene Israel as much members of their village community as of their caste group—perhaps more so, because their caste group happened to be a particularly dispersed one.[11] But the great possibilities of employment in the fast-developing city encouraged the formation of a sizeable group, leading to more complex relations between co-members. Furthermore, the presence within the same locality of different groups, speaking different languages and having different cultural forms, encouraged intra-group cohesion. In Bombay Bene Israel emerged as a community, a strongly knit kind of group bound together by their common life.

RELIGIOUS REVIVAL

Moreover, Bene Israel religious life flourished in Bombay: synagogues were built; periodicals devoted to instruction in the principles and practices of Judaism came into being; books of Jewish interest were translated into Marathi, the mother tongue of the Bene Israel, and so on. Furthermore, Bene Israel began to refer to themselves as 'Jew caste'.[12]

This second religious revival of the Bene Israel was assisted by the arrival of a small group of Cochin Jews in 1826 who, like David Rahabi, devoted themselves to the teaching of Judaism, but this time in a professional capacity.[13] Kehimkar writes, 'These Cochin Jews were teachers, preachers and expounders of the Law. During the working days of the week they taught the children, and in the meetings held on Sabbaths, they read and explained the Bible to the people, as was done by the sage Ezra during the time of the Second Temple.'[14]

Paradoxically the Bene Israel religious revival was fostered by their encounter with the missionaries. The ban on missionary activities in India was lifted in 1813; education presented the most fruitful field for the missionaries' labours, and their schools soon attracted the Bene Israel. In 1827 the American Mission established a Hebrew school at Alibag, in the Konkan, attended by thirty Bene Israel children of whom eight were girls. In 1829 there were some 130 Bene Israel children in the schools run by the American Mission. In 1836 some 250 Bene Israel children, of whom one-third were girls, attended the schools of Dr John Wilson of the Scottish Presbyterian Mission—startling figures for a time when illiteracy was high and the Bene Israel were new to book-learning. (And these figures do not include the Bene Israel attending the schools of other missions.) As the total Bene Israel population in the 1830s could not have exceeded 6,000, it is clear that a substantial part of the Bene Israel children were attending school. In 1842 as many as thirty Bene Israel were attending Dr Wilson's College in Bombay.

The missionaries' Marathi translation of the Bible[15] proved a tremendous boon; for the first time the Bible reached the Bene Israel in a language with which all were familiar, 'thereby,' Bene Israel acknowledge, 'greatly indebting them to the translators'. Again, one of the first actions of Dr John Wilson was the publication of a Hebrew-Marathi grammar for the Bene Israel; and to him also is due the introduction of Hebrew into the syllabus of the matriculation and higher examinations of the Bombay University.

But, Bene Israel insist, 'in spite of the missionaries' intense efforts, there were but very few conversions. When it came to the acceptance of the messiahship of Jesus, our Bene Israel just knew that the missionaries were wrong and simply closed their minds.'

Again: 'But it wasn't all one-sided: the missionaries needed teachers for their schools, for which they found our Bene Israel useful.' And indeed, in the American Marathi Mission Report of 1826 I read that employment of Jewish teachers had been a good plan 'because Jews do not allow heathenish practices to be performed'.[16]

Growing knowledge of English brought the Bene Israel into contact with their co-religionists in the West: all kinds of Jewish publications from England and America began to find their way into the Bene Israel homes and put them in touch with the latest developments of Judaism; there was personal contact with Jews from the West visiting India; there were occasional Bene Israel visits to the West; the Anglo-Jewish Association of London heard of the Bene Israel and stretched out a helping hand, and so on.

A member of the community told me, 'Perhaps our people are right about the way they are explaining all this to you. But perhaps they talk such a lot about religion to you because they think it will interest and please you a lot. But they should make it clear that they were not only interested in learning English from the missionaries because then they could read the books about the Jewish religion written in English. They also wanted to learn English because people keen on education and advancement were learning English. And our Bene Israel are keen on education and advancement—as you must have noticed for yourself—so they wanted to learn English. It wasn't only religion that they were interested in.'

THE BAGHDADIS: 'THE HIGHER JEW CASTE'

The Baghdadis, Kehimkar relates, 'have never as a community done anything for the religious or educational welfare of the Bene Israel'.[17] Nevertheless, I suggest that the Baghdadis played an important part in the nineteenth-century religious revival of the Bene Israel—and not only because, being familiar with the minutiae of Jewish religious practices, they provided the Bene Israel with an example of Jewish orthodoxy.[18] For the Baghdadi community soon outstripped the Bene Israel in a number of ways. The leaders of the Baghdadi community pioneered in industry, providing employment for many thousands of people. They built museums and public libraries. They subsidized the religious, educational and charitable services of their community. Moreover, Bene Israel relate, 'The Baghdadis shared the privileges of the Europeans in India.'[19] Clearly at that time the Baghdadis enjoyed not only religious superiority, but also prosperity and prestige. Not surprisingly, then, Bene Israel claimed alignment with their highly placed co-religionists. Not surprisingly, then, Bene Israel religious life flourished in Bombay, emphasizing their oneness with the Baghdadis.

It might be of advantage to digress for a moment and examine the veracity of some of the Bene Israel historical memories—an examination which indicates that this is not an unfair interpretation of the group's orientation towards Judaism and their Baghdadi co-religionists in the nineteenth century.

Bene Israel claim that they were completely isolated from their co-religionists for some two thousand years—an isolation which, Bene Israel assert, accounts for their past orientation to the Hindu social system. Nevertheless, there is evidence for the view that Bene Israel isolation from their co-religionists was much less complete than their historical memories suggest.

For example, Maimonides speaks of the Jews in India, and it is generally assumed that he is referring to the Bene Israel.[20] Thus at least in the twelfth century the existence of the Bene Israel was not unknown to their co-religionists.

Again, it seems certain that Rahabi was not the only Cochin Jew to visit the Bene Israel before the nineteenth century. For Claudius Buchanan in his *Christian Researches in Asia* writes about his visit to Cochin:

The Black Jews communicated to me much interesting intelligence concerning their brethren the ancient Israelites in the East. . . . They recounted the names of many other small colonies resident in northern India, Tartary, and China, and gave me a written list of SIXTY-FIVE places. I conversed with those who had lately visited many of these stations, and were about to return again. The Jews have a never-ceasing communication with each other in the East. Their families indeed are generally stationary, being subject to despotic princes; but the men move much about in a commercial capacity; and the same individual will pass through many extensive countries. So that when anything interesting to the nation of the Jews takes place, the rumour will pass rapidly throughout all Asia.[21]

As soon as Buchanan came to Bombay he was approached by the Bene Israel who had heard of his talks with the Cochin Jews and wanted to discuss the prophecies of Isaiah with him.[22] It is true that Buchanan met both these Jewish groups in the early nineteenth century, at a time when contact with their Cochin co-religionists is admitted by the Bene Israel; however, Buchanan implies that contact between the Jewish groups in the East was of long standing, and, moreover, not infrequent. It would be difficult to believe that the Cochin Jews had considerable contact with many small, obscure Jewish groups in far-away places but were unaware of the existence of the Bene Israel who lived on the same coast-line as themselves.

Indeed, there is direct evidence for contact between the two Jewish communities on the west coast of India. For the first Bene Israel synagogue was erected in Bombay in 1796 and its founder, Samaji Isaji Divakar, went to Cochin as a matter of course in order to obtain there a Scroll of the Law without which no synagogue is complete. But how did the founder of the first Bene Israel synagogue in the late eighteenth century know that in Cochin he could obtain a Scroll of the Law if there had been no contact between the two Jewish groups until the nineteenth century?

Again, there is evidence that the Bene Israel were not as ignorant of Hebrew as is generally assumed. For in an old Bene Israel cemetery in the Konkan I noticed gravestones with Hebrew inscriptions dated 1715—proof that Bene Israel were then not unfamiliar with at least the rudiments of that language. But if, as seems certain, Rahabi met and taught the Bene Israel in the middle of the eighteenth century,[23] it seems difficult to account for the existence of Hebrew inscriptions some decades before his arrival—except on the assumption that the Bene Israel never entirely forgot Hebrew or that David Rahabi was not the first didactically inclined Jew to visit them.[24]

Closer examination of even the few data cited here thus strongly suggests that the Bene Israel were not as isolated from Jewry nor as ignorant of Judaism as their historical memories imply. But before the move to Bombay the group's habitual relations had been with the Hindus and Muslims. Bene Israel orientation towards Judaism and their Baghdadi co-religionists took place at a time when the latter entered the social environment of the former as a highly placed group—an orientation which the Bene Israel, not, unnaturally, represent as a rediscovery.

It might be argued that all the data imply is that the Bene Israel change in orientation was facilitated by the entry of their Baghdadi co-religionists into the social environment; but that the data do not imply that the change in orientation was connected with the position of their co-religionists in the social environment. However, there was more to their co-religionists' entry into the social environment of the Bene Israel than mere orientation of the latter to the former. For the Baghdadis soon made a serious attempt to establish that there was a vital difference between themselves and the Bene Israel, because 'pure Jewish blood does not flow in their veins', and refused to accord them 'pure' Jewish status. In a letter to *The Jewish Chronicle* in London Kehimkar complained of 'the unjust odium incurred by the community', the Bene Israel, 'in the eyes of their more favourably circumstanced co-religionists', the Baghdadis.[25] The attitude of the Baghdadis led to much strife between the two Jewish groups of Bombay.

An informant relates:

For decades the Baghdadi Jews did not count the Bene Israel in the quorum required for public worship: they would not call up Bene Israel worshippers to the Reading of the Law. As recently as 1934 or so, an unsuccessful attempt was made to exclude the Bene Israel from the use of beds reserved for Jews in the biggest hospital in Bombay. And in Rangoon the High Court had to intervene before the Bene Israel were accepted as members of the single local synagogue. The Bene Israel were irretrievably identified with the coloured subject peoples of India. The Baghdadi Jews, however, did not allow this to happen to themselves. Their aim was acceptance as equals by the white rulers of India, as will be evidenced by the attempt made as recently as 1933–35 in the British Parliament to get Baghdadi Jews included in the separate European electoral rolls for the Central and State Legislatures to be constituted under the Government of India Act, 1935.

The Bene Israel concern over the Baghdadi attitude justifies the interpretation put forward here of the Bene Israel nineteenth-century religious revival. For Jewish communities can exist side by side, in a repetitive fashion—as do the Ashkenazim and Sephardim in England.[26] Moreover, as indicated in the Introduction, from the point of view of Judaism the various communities are of equal status. Hence from the point of view of Judaism the Bene Israel had but little need to concern themselves with the Baghdadis who, as Dr E. Moses, a leading member of the Bene Israel community and former mayor of Bombay, complained in a letter to the *Jewish Advocate*, an Indian-Jewish paper, in February 1945, are 'always trying to pass on a White Man's ticket . . . are foremost in running down the Bene Israel', denying them 'pure' Jewish status.

Thus it is suggested here that the Bene Israel concern over the Baghdadi attitude makes sense only when considered in relation to the damage in Bene Israel status which the former ascribed to the attitude of the latter. Such an interpretation is corroborated by the change which the relations between the two communities have undergone in recent years. Though virtually all Bene Israel informants frequently complained about the Baghdadi attitude, many of them indicated that they could now afford to be less sensitive to Baghdadi criticism than before. 'In the new India all are equal. Now Baghdadis are no better than Bene Israel. Now all are equal. Now what does it matter?' Other informants referred to changes in the economic position of the Baghdadi community. 'Baghdadis could always get work in the Sassoon mills. But now the mills have been sold. Now all are equal.' Some informants said, 'Baghdadis don't seem to claim an exclusive title to the true creed these days. But this is not because Bene Israel are more orthodox now. It is because the Bhagdadis can no longer play the part of the higher Jew caste'—as elsewhere in India, where religious prestige is tied to secular power, loss of the latter tends to diminish the former. And indeed, some rights and obligations now blur the boundary between the two Jewish communities of Bombay. For example, some Bene Israel children are now being admitted to the Baghdadi communal school; during the last war Baghdadi invited Bene Israel to co-operate in defence activities rendered necessary by German anti-Jewish propaganda in India.[27]

One of a group of Bene Israel informants who described themselves as 'interested and yet detached observers of the whole sorry Bene Israel-Baghdadi business' said:

> We don't know whether you have realized that the relations between our two communities were not unlike those between castes. Baghdadis complained that we were assimilated and that therefore we could not be regarded as pure Jews. But they played the part of the superior Jew caste: they enjoyed prestige and wealth which they did not wish to share with us, and they justified themselves by referring to their superior spiritual dignity. Surely all this is alien to Judaism! Surely all this shows that they too were assimilated! Perhaps we are a little assimilated—but then so are other Jews, especially those who like us have good friendly relations with their non-Jewish neighbours. And we have been here for two thousand years, while they have become assimilated in a very short time.

When I asked these informants whether they held that Bene Israel determination to be accepted as pure Jews was the result of religious fervour only, I was told:

> You suspect that we were impressed not only by Baghdadi Orthodoxy but also by their great wealth and prestige. We are not saying that you are completely mistaken. But there was much more to it. It wasn't that our Bene Israel wanted to gain prestige by being associated with the Baghdadis, but that they feared to lose prestige by the Baghdadi attitude: because the Baghdadis made out that Bene Israel were a kind of Jewish half-caste or outcastes—and you must know by now what being outcastes means in India! Are you surprised our Bene Israel protested? Do you think that when the Baghdadis implied that we were not pure Jews they were motivated by concern for Judaism only? It was just an excuse! It was all an attempt to create the impression that pure Jews are all fair-complexioned. And yet there is in the whole world hardly any group more

mixed than the Jewish. In India alone intermarriage was made more difficult by the rigid caste system—which Bene Israel themselves enforced for a very long time. And so our Bene Israel are likely to be much less mixed than Jews elsewhere. No, it was all because the Baghdadis feared that they would lose prestige if they became associated with our Bene Israel community....

Louis Rabinowitz who visited Bombay in 1952 writes about the relations between the Bene Israel and Baghdadis:

It is only in recent years that they have been accepted as full Jews by the younger community of Baghdadi origin. They were not counted in Minyan, intermarriage with them was forbidden, and they did not benefit (nor do they now) from the trusts. . . . The facts were patently clear. Under the British Raj a white skin was an honour placing its owner in a privileged position. The greater the dissociation from Indian coloured Jews the better. With the attainment of independence by India, however, the tables have been decisively turned. It is the Indian who is 'top dog' now, and the formerly privileged class has hastened with almost indecent haste to welcome the Bene Israel as brothers and co-religionists! Naturally there are still some diehards, and need it be stressed that among them are some of the trustees?[28]

Clearly, then, the conflict has lost much of its significance in contemporary India. But this does not mean that it has disappeared. Indeed, the controversy about the religious status of the Bene Israel was exported to Israel and, for a time, waged with renewed vigour—contributing to the preoccupation with the problem of 'Who is a Jew?' (But even before the irruption of the Bene Israel controversy in Israel, some informants told me, 'While what these Baghdadis think is no longer all that important in India, they have many more ties with Jews outside India than we have, and so the Baghdadis can still influence the attitude of non-Indian Jewry towards our Bene Israel community.')

As has already been stated in the Introduction, a superior-inferior relationship between Jewish communities differing widely from one another is by no means unusual. But while the superior-inferior relationship between the German Jews and the Jews from Eastern Europe reflected a secular inequality—for example, German Jews simply did not wish to marry into a group so unhappily underprivileged, so below them in professional attainments and economic circumstances as the Jews from Eastern

Europe—a new feature enters into the unequal relationship between the Jewish communities of India. If there is no inter-marriage between the Jewish communities of India, this is an expression of religious inequality. In other words, to the distinction of secular status is added that of religious dignity.

Nor is this surprising. For whatever differences there are between them, Jews, being a minority group, tend to share a common status within the host society. Hence it is not unusual for an established Jewish community to resent the influx of co-religionists whose traits may be evaluated as lower, fearing that the newcomers may adversely affect the status of Jews. The established Jewish community may try to find openings for its co-religionists in other countries or it may nurse the newcomers over the period of transition, helping them to adopt the traits which are symbols of higher status. But in India, in comparison with the lower communities, the higher communities are newcomers; the differences between them—in colour, occupation, wealth, prestige, influence, and so on—are probably much greater than the differences between Jewish communities elsewhere in the Diaspora; moreover, the main difference, being physical, is doomed to be permanent. Unwilling to share a common status with the older communities, the newcomers repudiated the unity and equality of Indian Jewry, considering themselves as existing in a higher degree of religious perfection. Such a situation is of course alien to Judaism. But because it was very much in consonance with the dominant Hindu system and because, moreover, the old communities, isolated for centuries from the mainstream of Jewish life, did not *at first glance* conform to the image of Jews, the claim of the newcomers met with some success.

NOTES

1. For example, in Psalms 87: 4; 89: 11.
2. B. J. Israel, ibid. p. 3.
3. Kehimkar, ibid. p. 40, footnote by Dr I. Olsvanger.
4. Kehimkar, ibid. p. 41. The Rahabi family came to Cochin from Aleppo in the middle of the seventeenth century and soon played an important part in Cochin Jewry. (Pereyra de Paiva mentions the family in his

Notisias dos Judeos de Cochim, Amsterdam, 1686.) For many years the Rahabi family acted as agents of the Dutch East India Company.

5. Kehimkar, ibid. p. 41.
6. Among Arabs, *kadi*, or *cadi*, meaning judge, is used for both religious and civil judges; and it has been suggested that the use of an Arabic term for so important an office supports the view (referred to in Chapter 2) that the Bene Israel came to India from an Arab country.
7. Kehimkar, ibid. pp. 45–6.
8. Kehimkar, ibid. p. 47.
9. For example, Kehimkar, ibid. p. 43, writes, 'The date on the *latest* [my italics] Sanad of the Jhiratkar family which authorized them to act as Kajis was 1770.' And it appears that *Sanads* were but rarely renewed.
10. Many Bene Israel told me, 'Our ancestors were the soldiers of the British.' Kehimkar, ibid. p. 218, writes, 'In fact the Bene Israel soldiers were the pink of the Native Army of the Bombay Presidency, and constituted almost half of the number of native officers of each regiment of the Bombay Presidency for nearly a century and a half.' However, the introduction of a system of grouping regiments according to caste eventually forced most of them to relinquish military service: there were not enough of them to form a regiment of their own. Moreover, an informant said, 'Bene Israel in the army were like cork in water— they simply had to come to the top; there was no help. And so there would have had to be a regiment solely of officers for Bene Israel would not be content to remain privates.'
11. Srinivas in *Religion and Society among the Coorgs of South India*, pp. 31–2, describes the structural situation in India as subject to opposed types of solidarity. On the one hand, '. . . members of the same caste living in different villages have a great deal in common'. On the other hand, '. . . members of a village community, whatever their caste, have certain interests in common'. Srinivas terms the solidarity of the caste 'horizontal solidarity', the solidarity of sections of different castes occupying different positions in the hierarchy and living in one locality 'vertical solidarity'.
12. For example, Kehimkar, ibid. pp. 256, 257, cites letters written by the Bombay Bene Israel in the nineteenth century to government officials in which the community refers to itself as 'Jew caste or Israel caste'. It is not suggested here that the Bombay community dropped the name 'Bene Israel' entirely. But it is suggested that the term 'Jew caste' occurs often enough to be significant. (In the census reports, too, Bene Israel referred to themselves as 'Jews'.)
13. One wonders why these Cochin Jews came to settle among the Bene Israel. Was it that, tortured by poverty as many of them were, they were tempted by the prospect of finding employment as teachers and preachers among the Bene Israel? Kehimkar, ibid. p. 68, says of one of these Cochin teachers, 'He was intelligent, active and amiable. His appearance inspired reverence in and out of the community, and most persons saluted him as the High Priest of the Bene Israel. He served as a Hazan or Reader in the then newly-formed synagogue of the Bene Israel for the trifling sum of Rupees 100 per annum.' Did they do it for the sake of the prestige accorded to them by the Bene Israel? Had some of them fallen foul of their own community and preferred to settle elsewhere? Thus Kehimkar, ibid. p. 66, relates that one of these Cochin

Jews was a convert to Christianity; but 'his affections towards his brethren in the flesh, and once in faith, were not diminished. He opened for them the gates of religious and secular knowledge, by starting schools for their children. . . .' Perhaps the early nineteenth century was a time when going to teach Judaism among the Bene Israel was the fashionable thing to do. At any rate, in 1833 another two groups of Cochin Jews arrived among the Bene Israel of Bombay.

14. Kehimkar, ibid. p. 66. (Kehimkar's reference to the activities of Ezra in ancient times is in line with his tendency to establish similarities between the goings-on among the Bene Israel and the ancient Israelites.)

15. Genesis was translated into Marathi in 1819; Exodus in 1833. Bene Israel told me, 'This translation business was carried on very slowly. But once done, it could be obtained free or at a very trifling cost. And in spite of the general Christian tone of the interpolations, it was exceedingly useful.'

16. However, a later report states that some Hindu children were bringing idols to school—which was all the fault of their Jewish teachers.

17. Kehimkar, ibid. p. 56. Kehimkar adds however that Solomon David Sassoon and his nephew Jacob E. D. Sassoon 'have of late years shown the nobleness of their family and the magnanimity of their mind in studying the welfare of the Bene Israel, and have thereby set an excellent example to their country-men, who, we trust, will now take it to heart, and follow in their foot-steps'.

18. Informants told me, 'When Jews from Baghdad first came to settle in Bombay, their example fascinated the Bene Israel. The strict orthodoxy of the Baghdadis cast a glamour over them'. And Kehimkar, quoting from a letter he sent to *The Jewish Chronicle* in London in 1883, refuting the allegations made in that paper by 'some unkindly disposed' Baghdadis that 'pure Jewish blood does not flow in the veins of the Bene Israel', argues, ibid. pp. 50, 52,

> If the Bene Israel have lost caste in the sight of 'Pure Jews', it is difficult to understand how there could have existed the close communion there did between the Bene Israel and the Mesopotamian Jews when the latter came to settle in Bombay for commercial purposes. Nay, the communion between them was so strong that the latter had for some time no other place of resort than the kindly homes of the former. They received their religious privileges also in the synagogue of the Bene Israel and buried their dead in the Bene Israel cemeteries. . . .

However, 'close communion' between an established Jewish community and new Jewish arrivals is not unusual. Nor is it at all unusual for the latter to form a community of their own as soon as their numbers increase.

19. Many Bene Israel said, 'Is Baghdad in Europe then? The Baghdadis are no more Europeans than Bene Israel!' Some informants said, 'We too could have insisted that we are Europeans—because the British thought of Jews as Europeans. But our Bene Israel had no desire to pass on a White Man's ticket!' (However, a very knowledgeable and most trustworthy informant told me, 'The position of the Bene Israel sometimes gave rise to very absurd anomalies': Bene Israel girls went to schools which were avowedly for Indians, and competed for prizes which were reserved for those of purely Indian parentage; Bene Israel boys usually

went to schools for European and Eurasian boys; and again, both Bene Israel men and women in some departments of Government Service were unhesitatingly admitted into the European grade.)

20. 'But the Jews of India,' Maimonides wrote to the Rabbis of Lunel (a city in southern France, renowned as a seat of Jewish learning) at the end of the twelfth century, 'do not know the Written Law, except that they rest on Saturday and perform circumcision on the eighth day.' As the Jews of Cochin are known to have been familiar with the Written Law (the Law of Moses), the prophets, and parts of the Talmud, it is assumed that Maimonides was referring to the Bene Israel—'and other sources generally confirm this', writes Louis Rabinowitz, *Far East Mission*, Johannesburg, 1952, p. 76. However, B. J. Israel, ibid. p. 3, writes (in a footnote), 'Maimonides may have referred to some other isolated Jewish group in Afghanistan, Baluchistan or Eastern Persia, which were at the time under the rule of the Delhi Sultanate and which may in the Muslim Middle East have been included in the geographical region of India'. (But even if Maimonides was not writing about the Bene Israel, the suggestion that he knew of the existence of these distant, small, obscure Jewish communities in Afghanistan, Baluchistan or Eastern Persia, makes it even more likely that he was not unaware of the existence of the Bene Israel who lived on the west coast of India.)

21. Claudius Buchanan, *Christian Researches in Asia*, 4th ed., London, 1811, p. 225.

22. Buchanan, ibid. p. 233.

23. Rahabi was born in 1720.

24. I am referring to the Bene Israel cemetery in Nowgaon, the village near which the ancestors of the Bene Israel are believed to have been ship-wrecked. When I told Bene Israel informants that these Hebrew inscriptions are pre-David Rahabi, they replied, 'That's what you say! According to our tradition he came many centuries ago, so there is nothing to wonder about these inscriptions! Anyhow, we told you to go to Nowgaon, so that you could see the place where our ancestors landed. As for these gravestones, there was no need to go to out-of-the-way village for them: you will find them in other old Bene Israel cemeteries in the Konkan.'

25. Kehimkar, ibid. p. 50 (in the letter referred to in footnote 18 above.)

26. Ashkenaz has since the tenth century been identified with Germany. As the German and North French Jews formed a uniform group in culture and ritual, they were called Ashkenazim in contradistinction to the South European or Sephardi Jews. Until the expulsion from France in the fourteenth century, Northern France was the centre of the Ashkenazim; then Germany took its place and from the middle of the sixteenth century Eastern Europe. There are further divisions within each group on the basis of place of origin. True, there has been a certain loss of community consciousness among the British-born descendants of these immigrants; but at one time diversities in place of origin had vital implications for social relationships in such matters as the choice of a husband or wife, and there was much ridicule of the differences in character and skill; nevertheless, these communities were not ranked—and certainly not on religious lines.

27. An informant said, 'I don't suppose there are very many Bene Israel who realize just how clever it was of the Baghdadis to invite us to participate in these defence activities. The German propaganda said that Jews were

E

aliens in India. So the Baghdadis could point to the Bene Israel and say to the Indians, "Look at our Bene Israel brethren—do they look like aliens to you?"'

28. Rabinowitz, ibid. pp. 71–2. *Minyan* (literally 'number') is the minimum required for community prayers, that is, ten male Jews above the age of thirteen. Again, trusts for the Jewish poor, from which the Bene Israel were excluded, were set up by the leaders of the Baghdadi community. Intermarriage between Bene Israel and Baghdadis is still frowned upon by the latter. Certainly it is very rare indeed.

5

The 'Visibility' of the Bene Israel

COMMUNITY CONSCIOUSNESS

All Bene Israel are in frequent contact with non-Bene Israel. Many Bene Israel are in intimate contact with non-Bene Israel. Some spend more time with non-Bene Israel than with Bene Israel. A few speak slightingly of the community and try to isolate themselves from co-members. Nevertheless, Bene Israel do seem to feel that common historical memories, common religion, common fate, common traditions, bring them together on a level different from that on which they associate with members of other groups. In comparison with this sense of community, non-Bene Israel, even those whom they know well and meet often and think highly of, tend to be strangers.

Some Bene Israel are doubtful about the desirability of this sense of community, 'It may be all right for strong and important communities—but what do our Bene Israel get out of remaining apart?' Again, some Bene Israel, very much aware of the Government's wish for a reduction of community consciousness, plead that this sense of community is not confined to Bene Israel 'and so our Bene Israel should not be blamed for it'; moreover, they insist that Bene Israel community consciousness does not involve hostility to non-Bene Israel nor does it result in diminution of their loyalty to Indian society. (The Government's wish is for a reduction of communal isolation: the Indian constitution guarantees preservation of minority cultures.) On the other hand, some Bene Israel complain that recent times have brought a weakening of community consciousness. But whether they approve or disapprove of it, it is agreed that this sense of community is unlikely to meet with sudden death.

Indeed, many Bene Israel—even those who try to isolate themselves from co-members—almost always introduce their information, even when it concerns purely personal matters, with 'we Bene Israel' or 'our community'. Again, they are apt to attribute this or that characteristic to their community.

PHYSICAL TYPE

Thus Bene Israel hold that it is easy to distinguish them by their appearance. Kehimkar writes:

> As the Bene Israel differ from the people around them in physiognomy, bodily structure and general appearance, they can easily be distinguished in the midst of a multitude of others. The typical Bene Israel is from five feet to five and a half feet in height and is usually well-built. The mien of a Bene Israel is frequently warlike. The complexion on his face is fair and his body generally well proportioned and tending to be spare rather than corpulent. His features are usually somewhat elongated, and wear a pleasing expression of intelligence and of firmness of character. His nose is straight, his lips are thin and his cheeks full and fair. The colour of his eyes is dark brown. His hair is of deep black. Some, it is true, possess a somewhat lightly coloured hair; but this is generally to be seen in children. . . . The insteps of their feet are generally high, and they do not tattoo their bodies like their Hindu neighbours.
>
> Bene Israel women are generally good-looking and fair. Though in some cases beauty has faded owing to poverty, their original Israelitish features survive. They can easily be recognized from Hindu women. They are very active and have lively black eyes. They have straight noses and thin lips. Their hair is black, but occasionally of a somewhat light colour. The insteps of their feet are high. Like Hindu women they wear their hair tressed up in a knot behind their heads; but they do not tattoo their bodies like their Hindu neighbours.[1]

'Clearly,' many Bene Israel insist, 'there is a great deal of Jewish physiognomy to be recognized in our people, showing that we are of Abrahamic race and therefore pure Hebrews in origin.' But in spite of their insistence on their Jewish physiognomy, they cannot 'easily be distinguished in the midst of a multitude of others': *Like Jews everywhere*, Bene Israel resemble in physical features the people among whom they have been living for many centuries; there are no racial traits that belong to Jews universally.[2]

But this is neither here nor there: for in spite of all the evidence of history against the belief that Jews are a race, in spite of the fact that Jews show almost all the racial diversities from black to white, many Jews tend to think of themselves, and many non-Jews tend to think of them, as a race. This is possible because the racial differences among Jews are generally unknown—Jews of a non-European type are comparatively few in number and, moreover, somewhat on the outer rim of Jewish life.[3] Bene Israel belief that they can 'easily be distinguished in the midst of a multitude of others' is part of the force that unites them; but having little of the looks commonly attributed to Jews emphasizes Bene Israel separateness from the main body of their co-religionists.[4]

DRESS

The Bene Israel dress in much the same fashion as do most other urban minorities and many urban Hindus: men wear European dress,[5] women wear the sari. Informants told me, 'Even the Bene Israel ladies whom you meet dressed in European style have saris and wear them from time to time.'[6]

An informant told me of a childhood experience, 'A cousin of mine, playing with Anglo-Indian friends, was once ashamed to admit that the sari-clad woman calling out for him was his mother —he said she was his ayah. I know of another Bene Israel family that described itself as "Anglo-Indian Jews" and was reluctant to receive relatives in Indian costume in its house.' But he insisted that such a reaction to conditions in British India was rare among the Bene Israel: 'The Bene Israel were irretrievably indentified with the coloured subject people of India and, in the main, were content to be so identified.'

Bene Israel women do not apply the *kunkoo*, the red mark on the forehead—'it is part of the Hindu religion and therefore sinful for Jews'.[7] I do not pretend to know whether the absence of the *kunkoo* is as important a distinguishing mark between Bene Israel and non-Bene Israel women as informants insist that it is.[8]

Baghdadi women wear European dress—though it is said they may acquire saris for fancy dress occasions. Thus, while dress does not separate Bene Israel from Indians, it does contribute to Bene Israel separateness from their co-religionists.

An informant said, 'There are no missing links, so to speak, from the original Indian dress to the full blown European costume: all stages of the transition are in full vigour among the Bene Israel. The little boy who was taken to the synagogue in a big town for the first time, was unconsciously struck by the humour of the situation, when he naïvely remarked, "How is it, mother, that in our Temple there are Hindus and Muslims, Parsis and Europeans as well as Jews?" He was referring to the different costumes.'

LANGUAGE

Marathi is the mother tongue of the Bene Israel, but very many of them also speak English. Some habitually speak in English and, it is said, as well as the educated Englishman. (Certainly a number of Bene Israel commented upon my difficulties in pronunciation; one member of the community informed me, 'In addition to your difficulty in enunciation, your grammar is uncertain and your vocabulary poor.')

A number of Bene Israel are attending classes in Modern Hebrew conducted by the Jewish Agency-subsidized teacher in Bombay. Some, especially those who lived in Israel for a time but returned because they felt unable to gain complete acceptance, know sufficient Hebrew for ordinary conversational purposes.

Thus Bene Israel are perfectly capable of communicating with their Marathi-speaking Indian neighbours and English-speaking co-religionists. Nevertheless, as many Baghdadis pointed out, while one is used to Jews speaking a European language or having one of the dialects of Arabic as a mother tongue, Marathi is a language generally foreign to Jews—thus the very knowledge of Marathi emphasizes Bene Israel alignment with a people foreign to the main body of Jewry.

NAMES

Kehimkar writes:

> It must have been in order to divest themselves of even the minutest vestiges of peculiarity in the eyes of the Natives, that the Bene Israel adopted Hindu names . . . But the practice of taking Hindu names has now almost ceased. Even while using

such names they at the same time retained also Biblical names
. . . which were used only on occasions of religious rites and
ceremonies. Again, sometimes they retained their Hebrew
names in ordinary intercourse with their gentile neighbours but
in such cases usually made slight changes in them, to make
them correspond with those of the Hindus.[9]

Had the ancestors of the Bene Israel not devised this plan for
adapting themselves in matters indifferent to the practice of their
neighbours, Kehimkar argues, they would probably have run the
risk of extermination: their prudence and foresight in this matter
cannot but command one's admiration.'[10]

Considering that Bene Israel, unlike so many other Jewish
communities, have never experienced persecution but have lived
for many centuries on excellent terms with their Indian neighbours, it does seem somewhat unfair of Kehimkar to explain Bene
Israel Indianization to fears of otherwise being exterminated.
Moreover, very many orthodox Jews adopt the names current in
the countries in which they find themselves, using their biblical
names only on occasion of religious ceremonies. But, then, what
Kehimkar—addressing a Jewish audience unaccustomed to co-
religionists having Indian names, wearing Indian dress, speaking
an Indian language, and so on—is trying to do is to make
palatable not general assimilation but Indianization.

Nowadays Bene Israel have biblical personal names and
biblical surnames—usually the father's name or grandfather's
name is treated as the surname.[11] A few also have English personal names. Bene Israel also have Indian surnames which, as is
common in the Konkan, indicate the villages from which they
hail.[12] Kehimkar writes, 'e.g., men who resided in Kehim called
themselves Kehimkar, those who lived at Penn called themselves
Penkar'.[13] There is no suggestion that a common village surname
indicates kinship.

The great majority of Bene Israel use only their biblical surnames. Some, especially those who are very much involved in the
affairs of the world beyond the communal horizon, use their
Indian surnames. But there are a number of Bene Israel in very
senior positions in the civil service who use their biblical surnames just as there are a number of Bene Israel in very minor
positions who use their Indian surnames. Only one member of
the community volunteered the information that he used his

Indian surname deliberately, as a kind of insurance—'One never knows what may happen. . . .' 'But he and his wife,' informants insisted, 'will always, always try to play it safe: these two were just born that way! What to do?' Again, some asserted, 'If a few of our Bene Israel don't use their biblical surnames, it just so happened by accident and not through thinking about it and then coming to a cunning decision.'

AREAS OF SETTLEMENT

Some 10,000 of the 13,000 Bene Israel in India live in Greater Bombay. The remaining 3,000 Bene Israel in India form small groups in various parts of the country—in the Konkan, in Poona, in Delhi, and so forth. The great majority of the 7,000 Bene Israel living outside India are to be found in Israel. There is a small community resident in Pakistan;[14] a few have gone to England and Australia.

There are ties of friendship, blood and marriage between the various Bene Israel communities, particularly between the small, frequently tiny, communities resident in various parts of India and the main community in Bombay. And as travel is comparatively cheap, non-Bombay Bene Israel visit their friends and kinsfolk in Bombay from time to time. Again, small non-Bombay Bene Israel associations sometimes approach Bombay Bene Israel associations for financial assistance towards their various enterprises, for the loan of a ritual object such as a Scroll of the Law, and so on. Usually a non-Bombay association applying for assistance from a Bombay association will ask those in its midst who have friends and kinsfolk among the committee of the Bombay association that is being approached to initiate the matter. On the other hand, the Bombay Bene Israel community, being the only Bene Israel community which maintains a school, orphanage, charity and education funds, etc., may ask non-Bombay Bene Israel for contributions towards these undertakings. But as the funds of the various Bene Israel communities are exceedingly meagre, and committees generally chary of spending resources, such appeals for assistance are the result of feelings of fellowship, of consciousness of kind regardless of dispersion, rather than of expectations of much help.

Although there is no Bombay district which is inhabited by

Jews only, something like 7,800 of the 11,000 Jewish inhabitants of the town live within close reach, or at least within walking distance,[15] of one another. Indeed, I have often heard this area referred to as the Jewish communal neighbourhood. The area in which they live in fairly close concentration is the meeting point of a number of wards—Byculla, Nagpada, Mazgaon, Umarkhadi—in which many of the poor of the city live.

Of the 7,800 Jews in this area, 7,000 are Bene Israel; 800 are Baghdadis. Thus the great majority of the two communities live close together. There is, however, very little fellowship between them: Bene Israel and Baghdadis tend to think of themselves as members of their own communities rather than as part of the Jewish group as a whole.

The difficulty of obtaining accommodation in the overcrowded communal neighbourhood has forced some 1,500 Bene Israel to move from the communal neighbourhood into wards which are also inhabited by the poor of the town. They now live some two to three miles from the communal neighbourhood; some have moved as far as Parel.

Only a few of the wealthier Bene Israel have remained in the communal neighbourhood;[16] the rest have moved into more pleasant districts. Some 900 reside in the middle-class suburbs of the town; about a hundred live in the best residential areas of Bombay, Malabar Hill and Colaba.

Some 500 Bene Israel form small groups at the fringe of Greater Bombay and cannot truly be regarded as part of Bombay Jewry.

The rest of the Baghdadi community, together with the Jews from Europe, live in Malabar Hill and Colaba.

The following table indicates both the size of the various Jewish groups in Bombay and the type of area in which they live.

	Bene Israel	Baghdadis	European Jews
Communal Neighbourhood	7,000	800	—
Areas similar to the Communal Neighbourhood	1,500	—	—
Middle-class Suburbs	900	—	—
Best Residential Areas	100	100	100[17]

WITHIN COMMUNAL BOUNDARIES

Thus over two-thirds of the Bombay Bene Israel live fairly close together. Such spatial proximity facilitates the observance of many religious activities which require the participation of co-members. Indeed, it may fairly be said that observance of Jewish Law necessitates the close living together of its adherents. However, the clustering together of co-members is not unusual in Bombay. For the many religious and linguistic differences between the various urban groups encourages spatial proximity between co-members.

The great majority of Bene Israel live in large, overcrowded, insanitary buildings inhabited by many dozens of families. A home in such a building usually consists of but one room. Thus a family of eight or more members—father, mother, their unmarried children, and sometimes one married son and his wife and children[18]—may live in one not very large room, which in spite of the congestion is beautifully clean. In the area in which they live in close concentration one or two floors of such a huge building may be occupied by Bene Israel families. (The few wealthier Bene Israel families who have remained in the communal neighbourhood occupy somewhat larger homes in the smaller and better preserved buildings in this area.)

Those Bene Israel who have moved into other poor areas of the town are frequently to be seen in the communal neighbourhood. They visit their kinsfolk and friends there; they join in the social activities; they attend the synagogues; they hire the synagogue-hall and synagogue dishes for feasts following upon the performance of rites connected with major events in the individual life-cycle,[19] and so on. However, as some ritual activities require the attendance of at least ten male adult co-members in the home, friends and kinsfolk from the communal neighbourhood will visit those who have moved into other districts.

On the other hand, the wealthier Bene Israel do not spend much of their spare time in the communal neighbourhood. True, they go there to attend synagogue services[20] and for ritual activities connected with major events in the individual life-cycle. But they do not hold the receptions following upon these ritual activities in the synagogue-hall but invite kinsfolk and friends to their homes or to a club or restaurant in Malabar Hill or Colaba.

Nevertheless, the wealthier Bene Israel are frequently prevailed upon to interest themselves in communal affairs and are asked to help the less fortunate members of the community—just as the wealthier members of other Bombay communities are prevailed upon to interest themselves in the affairs of their less fortunate co-members. The wealthier Bene Israel are applied to for contributions towards communal undertakings, for help in the search for employment, for professional advice, and so forth.

Wherever they live, the entrance to the home is marked by the *Mezuzzah*—a metal or wooden tube which contains, written on parchment, the first two paragraphs of the *Shema*, the confession of the Jewish faith—the distinctive sign of the Jewish home.[21] The home contains an oil-lamp affixed to the wall or hanging from the ceiling which is lit on the eve of Sabbaths and festivals. Many Bene Israel homes are decorated with pictures depicting biblical scenes. Hebrew books, such as the daily prayer-book, the prayer-books for the various festivals, the Pentateuch, etc., usually with a translation in Marathi or English, occupy a place of honour in the home. The fact that two Bene Israel families derive part of their income, and several schoolboys their pocket-money, from the sale of such books, testifies to the active interest in Jewish literature.

There is sympathy and criticism, friendship and rivalry, between the members of the Bene Israel community; but above all there is an intense interest in the affairs of co-members. Everyone knows where his co-members live and what they are doing; everyone speculates as to the income others enjoy and whether it is wisely spent; everyone is aware of the contributions others are making to communal undertakings and believes that some are not giving as much as they should; and so on. People's observation is sharp and everything is commented upon endlessly. Thus though law is nowadays the concern only of the courts,[22] the community is by no means without forms of redress. Bene Israel say, 'If the community would punish offenders, then the Government would punish the community. Still, no one likes it when "people laugh"—and that the Government cannot forbid.' The sanction of public criticism, 'people will laugh', is indeed feared.

Thus the co-activities enjoined by Judaism, the obligations which membership of the community imposes and the forms of togetherness which it encourages, provide the bases for the various types of groupings that comprise the pattern of Bene Israel social structure.

NOTES

1. Kehimkar, ibid. pp. 89–90.
2. A member of the community writes, 'I have time out of number picked Bene Israel out in a crowd and found myself right. But I agree it is becoming increasingly hard. Indeed it is becoming increasingly difficult to distinguish Indians from different parts of India, which was once easy. The distinguishing features are psychosomatic and not purely physical—expression, bearing, etc. come into it.' However, Kehimkar's assertion that Bene Israel can easily be distinguished in the midst of a multitude of others was (like the rest of the book) addressed to his non-Indian co-religionists—who would find it exceedingly difficult to distinguish between Bene Israel and non-Jewish Indians. Similarly, there may be differences between the English Jew and the English Christian which —although they may be so intangible, vague, and tenuous as to escape precise definition—may help the Englishman to distinguish between the English Jew and the English non-Jew. On the other hand, a Frenchman coming to England would find himself unable to distinguish by appearance between the English Jew and the English Christian. There are no racial traits which can be found among all Jews.
3. An informant objects: 'This is a typically European view. The Western Jew is on the outer rim. The Jew in the Orient (including North Africa) the norm.' However, from the eleventh century onward, the homes of all but a handful of Jews were in Europe, until the New World was opened up and Jews settled in it, like those driven from Spain in the fifteenth and sixteenth centuries, who settled in South America and the West Indies, and those driven from Russia in the nineteenth century, who settled in the United States and the British Dominions. But the New World is culturally an extension of Europe. That is, for centuries the rallying-point of Judaism was in the West: and it is therefore exceedingly difficult to understand how the Western Jew could have been on the outer rim of Jewish life. (Today, it is true, the centre of Jewry is again in the East, in the Land of Israel.)
4. Baghdadi informants told me, 'There are some European Jews who disapprove of our attitude to the Bene Israel. But doesn't it strike you as very strange that it is much easier to distinguish between us and Bene Israel than it is to distinguish between Bene Israel and Hindus?' When I replied, 'But, then, it may well be much easier to distinguish between you and Central European Jews than it is to distinguish between you and the non-Jews of Baghdad,' they said, 'One can see that you are one of those European Jews who disapprove of our attitude towards the Bene Israel.'
5. However, I came across two Bene Israel men wearing Indian dress. They were non-Bombay Bene Israel spending a holiday in Bombay. They

said, 'Away from Bombay, too, Bene Israel men wear European dress. But Indian dress is so much cheaper. Also it is so much more patriotic. So we combine patriotism and cheapness, so we wear it.' (Some Bene Israel, listening to this conversation, afterwards told me, 'And perhaps they like to arouse attention—which they certainly did by coming to the synagogue in Indian dress. But don't let us be nasty!') Some Bene Israel men, those amongst the most sophisticated section of the community, wear Indian evening dress. I was told of one member of the community who was said to wear European evening dress.

6. One member of a family in which all the women wear European dress told me, 'We are a sophisticated family. And also it is more comfortable than sari—and I could see that you thought the same when you tried on the sari!' She added, 'It is not because of a wish to disguise being Indian. I am very proud of my colour'. Other informants, however, suggested, 'That family has always been very Anglo-Indian. That's why! But as you can see for yourself, most among us are not like that!'

7. Once, during a wedding ceremony, two Bene Israel women who had married Hindus entered the synagogue wearing the *kunkoo*. These two— sisters—did not usually attend synagogue services; but they attended this wedding ceremony because the bridegroom was a close kinsman. There was great anger. It had been taken for granted that they would attend the ceremony—'But was there any need to wear the *kunkoo*, reminding all that they had married out? It is shameless!' (However, the father of these women was rather unpopular with many Bene Israel —which may have contributed to the great indignation felt at his daughters' wearing the *kunkoo*.)

8. An informant writes: 'Neither Christians nor Muslims wear *kunkoo*.'

9. Kehimkar, ibid. p. 38. Again, Kehimkar relates, 'The names Dinah and Esther were not in use formerly amongst the Bene Israel, for the reason, no doubt, of the rape committed on the former by Shechem the son of Hamor the Hivite, whereas Esther was married to a Gentile, the Persian monarch Ahasveros. For these reasons some orthodox people still object to those names. The name Judah also was not in favour among the Bene Israel, owing probably to the grudge which the ten tribes of Israel bore towards the tribe of Judah. Now, however, they do not object to those names.' I have met no Bene Israel who could confirm this report of prejudice against the names Dinah, Esther and Judah—Kehimkar's great-granddaughter is called Esther. True, Kehimkar wrote in the nineteenth century and Bene Israel may by now have forgotten their past prejudice against these names. But I cannot help suspecting that Kehimkar's main aim is to emphasize his community's aversion to inter-marriage (hence the aversion to names like Dinah and Esther) and the strength of the belief in descent from the Ten Tribes of Israel (hence the aversion to the name Judah). One of my informants relates that his maternal grandmother, born perhaps in 1860 or so, was named Esther.

10. Kehimkar, ibid. p. 39.

11. The surname 'Israel' was commonly used in official records for all Bene Israel personnel in the British army. (I have heard it suggested that this practice prevented their being confused with Indian Christians.) An informant writes, 'The Army authorities treated it as the caste name. Many Indians use caste names as surnames.'

12. However, one family claims to have no village surname. In spite of many explanations, I never quite understood how this came about.

13. Kehimkar, ibid. p. 39. As was to be expected, Kehimkar does not relate this mode of taking surnames to Indian custom, but cites biblical instances—'Elija the Prophet, for example, is surnamed the Tishbite, from Tishbi, a town in Naphtali. Jesse the Beth-le-hemite . . . etc.' And he reminds his readers that Jews in Germany and Italy, and the White Jews of Cochin, too, tend to take surnames from the localities in which they find themselves.

14. Bene Israel went to Karachi in the nineteenth century. Many left after partition. In 1958 there were some 400 Bene Israel resident in Karachi.

15. I am tempted to say that they live within comfortable walking distance of one another. But this would be a most subjective statement: none of the people I came in contact with were fond of walking; they used transport even for distances which they admitted could well be walked.

16. There were four Bene Israel families in the communal neighbourhood about whom I was told that they could well afford to move into the more pleasant districts of the town. About six other families I was told, 'If they lived there, they might not be able to educate their children as expensively as they do now, because of higher rents elsewhere; so it is right that they stay where they are.'

17. Many of the few hundred European Jews who came to India in the nineteen-thirties later left the country.

18. Theoretically the Bene Israel household is a joint one. Nowadays, however, it is more often an elementary unit. The Bene Israel family will be discussed in some detail in chapter 7.

19. There is one place of worship outside the communal neighbourhood. But though the Bene Israel living in Parel, a poor area of Bombay, have their own prayer-hall, they have retained their membership in their synagogues in the communal neighbourhood. They use the Parel prayer-hall for services on Sabbaths and festivals, but tend to perform the ritual activities connected with major events in the individual life cycle in the communal neighbourhood. Bene Israel synagogues will be discussed in chapter 8.

20. Bene Israel living in Bandra, a middle-class suburb of Bombay, though they have retained their membership in their synagogues in the communal neighbourhood, met in the home of a co-member, a doctor and former mayor of Bombay, for services on New Year and the Day of Atonement.

21. The custom of the *Mezuzzah* is based on an injunction in Deut. 6:9 and 11:20.

22. The urban Bene Israel 'know their rights'; that is, they know that most communal rules are not enforceable in the Government courts.

Part II

THE BENE ISRAEL AND
THE WORLD BEYOND
COMMUNAL BOUNDARIES

6

Beyond Communal Boundaries

Obviously, the Bene Israel community does not circumscribe the lives of its members. Bene Israel form part of the extensive Jewish group; politically Bene Israel are part of the wider entity, of city and state; and virtually all Bene Israel earn their living, many educate their children, look after their health, obtain legal advice, borrow money, and so on, beyond communal boundaries. Moreover, I was told, 'All Bene Israel have friends among other communities—usually Hindus and Mohammedans, as often as not, Christians and Parsis as well—and they are very good friends.'

Clearly, then, Bene Israel—men, women, children—do not shut themselves off from contact with non-Bene Israel, they do not look upon non-Bene Israel as dangerous aliens: on the contrary, they are eager to accept association with them.

TIES WITH THE BAGHDADIS

Bene Israel fit into Bombay Jewry still as members of their community. For the many ethnic and cultural differences between Bene Israel and Baghdadis render their merging exceedingly difficult. Nevertheless, spatial proximity between the two Jewish communities of Bombay has had some practical consequences other than strife: some rights and obligations blur the boundary between Bene Israel and Baghdadis.

For example, there are two occasions when Bene Israel invite Baghdadis to participate in the performance of religious rites. For as Bene Israel have no priests—descendants of Aaron, the first High Priest—in their midst, they invite a priest of the Baghdadi community to perform the 'Redemption of the First-born Son' (the ceremony is enjoined in Exodus 13: 13, 15) and to pronounce the 'Blessing of the Priest' was one of the features of the service

F

in the Temple at Jerusalem; it has been transferred into the service of the synagogue.

In the first case, the father engages a Baghdadi priest to perform the ceremony—indigent Baghdadi priests are only too glad to perform the 'Redemption of the First-born Son' in return for the traditional fee to which this entitles them.[1] 'This ceremony,' Kehimkar relates, 'has but recently been introduced among the Bene Israel. When there is no Cohen, the ceremony is omitted.'[2] In the second case, the committee of the Bene Israel synagogue invites a Baghdadi priest to pronounce the 'Blessing of the Priest' during the synagogue service on the Holy-days—for which Bene Israel informants claimed that he was paid although payment is not customary among other Jewish communities.[3] This ceremony, too, has only recently been introduced; where there is no priest the ceremony is omitted. From the Jewish point of view, if the first-born son is not redeemed he nevertheless retains his membership of the religious group; again, the omission of the 'Blessing of the Priest' does not invalidate the service.

This one-sided dependence—for Baghdadis do not require the ritual services of the Bene Israel—does not reflect a mystic, pre-ordained inequality in rights and duties. It is purely empirical and fortuitous that Bene Israel happen to have no priests in their midst: perhaps there were no priests among the small Jewish group which landed in the Konkan over a millennium ago; perhaps the priestly families lost their social identity or became extinct.

Again, Bene Israel are not the only Jewish community without priests in their midst.[4] Nevertheless, it has been suggested that their want of priests proves that they are not 'pure' Jews. Dr E. Moses, in a letter to the *Jewish Advocate*, writes:

> . . . I am sorry Chaplain Horowitz has entered into this controversy. He says the presence or absence of priests is the best test available. Whenever the *Birkath Cohanim* (Priestly Blessing) was pronounced by the priests in the synagogue in Karachi he did not find even one Bene Israel priest among the half a dozen priests from the Iraqians, Iranians or Russian Jews, and therefore the Bene Israel are not pure Jews. I must tell Chaplain Horowitz that there is a legend among the Bene Israel that the families of Bhorapkers and one or two others belonged to the priestly class. But their claims were rejected by the Com-

munity for want of proof. I am afraid that I am striking at the very root of the question when I ask the Chaplain how did he know that these men really belonged to the tribe of Levi and were not a fraud on the Community? The answer will be because they say so and because they observe Biblical injunctions prescribed for the priests which I must tell you are not so difficult to observe.... These are not the days for taking everything as Gospel truth....[5]

An informant asked why Bene Israel rejected the claims of the Bhorapker family, preferring to employ Baghdadi priests, said, 'Some of us don't believe in this claim of theirs to priestly descent, but the Baghdadis believe in their priests! And why shouldn't we employ Baghdadi priests? Besides it proves that they really know we are pure Jews—else would they perform the priestly ritual for us?'

While the relations arising from the 'Redemption of the First-born Son' and the 'Blessing of the Priest' involve the Bene Israel community and individual Baghdadis, there are relations in other fields which involve the Baghdadi community and individual Bene Israel.

For example, as there are but few Baghdadis in the teaching profession, some Bene Israel teachers are employed in the Baghdadi school; indeed, a member of the Bene Israel community acts as headmaster of the Baghdadi school. (This headmaster has now retired. However, this is not the first time that a member of the Bene Israel community has acted as headmaster of a Baghdadi educational undertaking. For Kehimkar, writing at the end of the nineteenth century, relates that the Baghdadis 'who at one time claimed to be the teachers of the Bene Israel are now taught under the Headmastership of Mr Joseph Ezekiel, a Bene Israel'.[6] Nowadays, too, Bene Israel act as examiners of Hebrew in the Bombay matriculation examination and as professors of Hebrew at one of the Bombay colleges.)

Again, Baghdadis admit some Bene Israel children to their school—although by no means as many as apply for admission.[7] Indeed, some Bene Israel alleged that a *numerus clausus* is imposed upon their children in the Baghdadi school.[8] Baghdadis have no wish to send their children to the Bene Israel school; in any case, the medium of instruction in the Bene Israel school is Marathi, the mother tongue of the Bene Israel, with which

Baghdadis are not familiar. The medium of instruction in the Baghdadi school is English.

There is some co-ordination of activities in matters which affect the circumstances of both communities. For example, Bene Israel and Baghdadis co-operate in Zionist activities—a co-operation encouraged by the Israeli attitude. '*Vis-à-vis* Israel,' an informant told me, 'the Bombay Zionists are Jews and not Baghdadis and Bene Israel.' Nevertheless, the Jewish Agency-subsidized teacher in Bombay must often organize separate activities for Bene Israel and Baghdadis.

Some years ago, an American rabbi visiting India, in an attempt to help overcome the estrangement between the two communities, persuaded some Bene Israel and Baghdadi youth to come together in club activities. But while the club is open to the youth of both communities, the majority of its members are Bene Israel.

Bene Israel and Baghdadis can visit each other's places of worship. A few members of the Bene Israel community occasionally attend the services in the Baghdadi synagogue,[9] but they are not invited to participate actively in the services. 'But when the Baghdadis first came to Bombay,' I was told, 'they were allowed, nay invited, to take an active part in the services of the Bene Israel synagogue. Nowadays, of course, they have their own places of worship, so they don't need to come to ours. But even now we would offer them an active part in the services whenever they wanted it. And you have seen that we always give the Baghdadi priests very much honour whenever they come to our Bene Israel services.'

Bene Israel who observe the Jewish dietary regulations—most of those who live in the communal neighbourhood as well as some of those who have moved into Malabar Hill and Colaba and into the middle-class suburbs of Bombay—buy meat from the Baghdadis. But although there are no Bene Israel butchers' shops,[10] the community is in no way dependent upon the Baghdadis for its meat supply. For a number of Bene Israel, particularly the Readers and Assistant-Readers of the synagogue, know how to slaughter animals according to the Jewish rites; and as it is cheaper, some Bene Israel prefer to buy an animal in the bazaar— a chicken or, for weddings, etc., a goat—and ask one of the Readers or Assistant-Readers of the synagogues to slaughter it rather than pay a higher price in the Baghdadi shop. (I am told that in olden times every male was taught the technique of ritual slaughter; this continued to be done by Bene Israel living outside the large centres of Jewish concentration until fairly recent times.) But Bene Israel admit that 'it is much simpler to walk into a Baghdadi shop and buy meat there. Besides, some Baghdadis deliver—which is simpler still!'

Some marriages between Bene Israel and Baghdadis have taken place. I know of two members of the Bombay Bene Israel community who have married Baghdadi girls (however, I am told there are more than two cases). An informant told me, 'it is a good thing in one way; but on the other hand, Baghdadi girls demand a much higher standard of living than our Bene Israel girls. They are more demanding, and so not many Bene Israel would be able to provide for Baghdadi wives.' Two Baghdadis have married Bene Israel girls—but the position of these two Baghdadis is such as to enable them to disregard co-members' criticism.[11]

Thus common religion has given rise to some co-activities between Bene Israel and Baghdadis; and though these co-activities do not spirit away the tension between the two Jewish groups of Bombay, they do help to control it.

TIES WITH COCHIN JEWRY

There is nowadays but little contact between the Bene Israel and the Jews of Cochin. A Cochin Jew is employed as Reader in one of the Bene Israel synagogues; a member of the Bene Israel community, an army officer stationed in Cochin, is often invited into the homes of the White Jews of Cochin. But the interests of Cochin Jewry—particularly of the Black Jews who form the majority—centre upon Israel;[12] a great number has left already and others are awaiting their turn to go to Israel.

TIES WITH NON-INDIAN JEWRY

The belief in the oneness of the extensive Jewish group supports some co-activities between Bene Israel and their non-Indian co-religionists. Thus the Bene Israel communal school receives an annual grant of some £350 from the Anglo-Jewish Association of London. (Bene Israel informants related that after Indian

Independence the Anglo-Jewish Association wished to stop the annual grant to the School. 'But we pointed out that India was still part of the British Commonwealth and so Anglo-Jewry should not forsake the School and so it was agreed to continue the grant. Were it not for the regular help received from the Anglo-Jewish Association, things would be even more difficult for our School.') Again, many Bene Israel have contributed to appeals in aid of the State of Israel. On the other hand, members of the Bene Israel community who wish to emigrate to Israel receive financial assistance from the Jewish Agency;[13] representatives of the main Bene Israel associations are invited to some of the social functions at the Israeli Consulate in Bombay;[14] and so on.

POLITICAL TIES

While Bene Israel fit into Bombay Jewry still as members of their own community, they enter the Indian political unit as citizens. Nevertheless, there are some occasions when the Government recognizes communal groupings.[15] For example, members of the various communities employed in Government offices are allowed to stay away from work on their most important festivals. (The festivals of the larger communities are, of course, public holidays on which all, regardless of communal membership, stay away from work.) Again, the Government makes some financial contribution towards some of the communal associations organized for educational purposes. But as such grants are intended to further the education of citizens rather than of members of the communities, the Government stipulates that the communal associations receiving such grants should be open to all regardless of communal membership—an unnecessary stipulation in the case of the Bene Israel whose school and girls' sewing class have always admitted children of all communities not only to fee-paying but also to free places. (During my stay in Bombay there were 756 children in the Bene Israel school of whom 269 were non-Bene Israel.)

Only a few Bene Israel take an active interest in political affairs. Thus during the disturbances over the possession of Bombay only three of my informants got excited over the issue, one of them so aggressively as to get injured in a fight. However, some said that as Bene Israel hailed from the Konkan, which forms part of

Maharashtra, they felt sympathy with the aspirations of Maharashtrans in the struggle for Bombay.

Many Bene Israel take immense pride in the image of moral superiority enjoyed by some Indian leaders, but they are not politically involved. I did not get the impression that informants were merely careful in their political utterances, but rather that they held that politics are the concern of the educated and the wealthy; others—involved in the strenuous struggle for economic survival as they are—had best leave politics alone.

FRIENDSHIP

An informant said, 'However many activities some of our Bene Israel like to carry out within the community, you will not find Bene Israel without friends among non-Bene Israel. All our Bene Israel have friends among members of other communities.'

Indeed, almost every member of the community I met sooner or later mentioned having non-Bene Israel friends, usually neighbours and fellow-workers. Certainly Bene Israel and non-Bene Israel associate freely: the men go about together; women visit back and forth with little gifts and offers of assistance; children play together. Occasionally a Hindu or Muslim may become so closely attached to one of the Bene Israel households that a newcomer may find it difficult to disentangle Bene Israel from non-Bene Israel. Thus on one occasion my host's friend provided me with such a detailed commentary on a ceremony that I could not refrain from complimenting him on his superior knowledge of his community's customs. In reply he told me that he was not a member of the Bene Israel community—he was a Muslim; but he was so attached to his Bene Israel friends that he spent most of his leisure hours in close association with them, whence his knowledge of their customs.

Some informants rarely let slip an opportunity to tell me that they much preferred their non-Bene Israel friends to Bene Israel. The commonest reason for preferring non-Bene Israel friends is that they are not quarrelsome and jealous as Bene Israel are, but kind and gentle as friends should be. Thus, as in all communities, there are grievances between members, and from these grievances some proceed to generalize about the inability of Bene Israel to be good friends.

On the other hand, a number of informants (especially those who held that they ought to provide not only information but also interpretation) were quick to point out that it was not that members of the community were incapable of friendship—'if that was the case, then we would not be so popular among other communities'—but that they were obliged to participate in so many activities providing scope for disagreement that it made stable friendships exceedingly difficult. 'Occasionally our Bene Israel may have to disagree about how to look after the community's affairs: how to look after the synagogue, the orphanage, the school, and so on. Brothers may quarrel, cousins may quarrel. It is difficult to avoid sometimes. What to do? But there are not so many opportunities for quarrelling with persons from other communities. They are not our brothers and cousins; they do not sit on our community's committees. Besides, persons from other communities who want to quarrel with us we can avoid—but one cannot always avoid quarrelsome Bene Israel.' Again, some stressed that it was 'very wrong to run down the community. Many Bene Israel are good friends with each other! And we often heard Bene Israel who have moved into other districts tell you how sad they are about not having Bene Israel neighbours; especially on festivals they feel very lonely. The truth of the matter is that we have been so fortunate as to find the various communities of India well disposed towards us and that is why we have friends among other communities—and not because our Bene Israel are incapable of being good friends with one another. Besides, to go about with persons from other communities makes a nice change!'

While non-Bene Israel friends may be invited to dinners, parties and picnics, they are excluded from synagogue services. This is not due to a feeling that they would not be interested, but seems based on a belief that it is wrong and that Judaism prohibits the presence of non-Jews during synagogue services.[16] Indeed, many Bene Israel were astonished when told that in England non-Jews were allowed to attend. As usual some said, 'How very unfair: Bene Israel are supposed to be lacking in orthodoxy—and then it turns out that we are much more orthodox than those who doubt us!' However, there is no objection to non-Jews viewing the synagogue before and after the services. Moreover, on one occasion when a Hindu friend of mine very much wanted to be present at a service, it was decided that this could be accomplished by opening the door to a room adjoining the synagogue and allowing him to watch from there. (This, I was told later, was rather unusual. Some assured me that it had been arranged as a favour to me. But I could not help suspecting that it had also been done in deference to the high position of this non-Jewish visitor. Indeed, one informant said, 'You handled this very badly: you just said to your friend, "Well, you will have to go now." You didn't think of the consequences this could have for our Bene Israel! Suppose he went and complained to Nehru about the lack of courtesy shown to him?') However, non-Jewish friends are allowed to attend the marriage ceremonies traditionally performed in the synagogue. Again, non-Jewish friends are allowed to attend ceremonies in the synagogue hall and in the home.

EARNING AND SPENDING

Some forty Bene Israel are employed by the community: they work as readers and assistant-readers, clerks and beadles, in the Bene Israel places of worship; as teachers and clerks in the communal school; as superintendent and cook in the communal home for orphans and destitutes; as clerks in the communal Co-operative Banking Society; and as officials in the communal cemetery. Two Bene Israel are employed in one of the prayer-halls as part-time teachers of Hebrew to the children of the congregation. (In the other Bene Israel places of worship it is the duty of the Readers and Assistant-Readers to instruct the children of the congregation in Hebrew. However, in one of the Bene Israel synagogues a member of the congregation has for some years now spent his evenings instructing the children in Hebrew without charging for his services. The president of this synagogue told me, 'It is most unusual! He won't even accept a present in appreciation of his services. But he is not married and loves children—which may explain all.') Two Bene Israel obtain part of their income from the sale of Hebrew books and religious prerequisites to members of the community.

There are a few Bene Israel in businesses of their own: three Bene Israel have printing businesses; five Bene Israel work as self-employed tailors; a few work as self-employed carpenters; one member of the community owns a bookshop. But these are very modest undertakings, and, moreover, not often patronized by co-members. Even the shirts and blouses distributed to the poor of the community before the festivals are made by non-Bene Israel tailors because they will work for less money than will Bene Israel tailors; even the communal associations will employ Bene Israel printers only if their prices are at least as low as those of non-Bene Israel printers. Some argued, 'Perhaps it is because so few members of our community are in businesses of their own that we just aren't used to dealing with Bene Israel businessmen; besides, being so very poor, our people feel that they must go where prices are lowest.' Only two Bene Israel are in large business undertakings of their own.

Some Bene Israel businessmen complained about not being supported by members of the community. On the other hand, they rarely employ co-members. Even Bene Israel working as managers in large concerns do not always care to take on co-members—'because they tend to take advantage and won't always obey orders of their Bene Israel superiors'. Similarly, I was told, 'If you want to help some poor Bene Israel widows by getting them positions as cooks in some Bene Israel households it is also very difficult: they just will not behave as cooks should behave but as equals.' Certainly the egalitarian values of the Bene Israel make it exceedingly difficult to enter into and accept philosophically a relationship of inequality between co-members.

Bene Israel estimate that ten per cent of the community earn a living in carpentry. 'It is not a good thing to be a carpenter—carpenters are very poor and lack education.' Indeed, whenever Bene Israel wish to indicate that a man is unworthy of notice, they are apt to say 'He is a carpenter'—uneducated, unsuccessful, noisy, and quarrelsome. (Nevertheless, I was told that Bene Israel carpenters used to be celebrated all over Bombay and were in evidence wherever specially skilled artisans were wanted. 'But they lacked enterprise and organization to set up for themselves an independent business which would have improved their position to a great extent. Perhaps it was due to want of capital that many an able carpenter had to drudge and toil for a master for a tiny sum a day, when he was capable of being a master workman, and thus a unit of some importance in the community due to self-confidence and self-respect that spring from a spirit of independence and power.')

On the other hand, Bene Israel estimate that 'some ten per cent of the community have forsaken the beaten path and through enterprise and initiative have established themselves in the professions such as medicine, law, and engineering'. However, the majority of Bene Israel are employed as clerks in Government and private offices or in equivalent positions—'which if not lucrative is at least respectable and secure'. Not surprisingly, then, Bene Israel tend to refer to themselves, and are frequently referred to by their Indian neighbours, as a clerk caste. Indeed, some Bene Israel who had heard that Jews elsewhere were frequently in businesses of their own exclaimed, 'How very strange! How very unlike Jews to go into business!'

Except for the small number of women who work as doctors, teachers, headmistresses, social workers, nurses and midwives, and a few, such as childless widows, who although untrained are forced to earn their own living, the income of the Bene Israel is earned by the menfolk. Bene Israel say, 'If a woman is trained for a profession, then it is perfectly respectable for her to follow it. But most Bene Israel women are not trained for the professions and a respectable caste does not send its untrained women out to work unless it is absolutely necessary—because untrained women at work may get into mischief.' And although everyone agrees that Bene Israel women are not inclined towards mischief, 'it is much better to leave well alone. Besides, Bene Israel girls are expected to help in the home, and anyhow they marry very early, in their late teens, so when should they go out to work?'

But if the majority of Bene Israel earn their living beyond communal boundaries, they also prefer to spend it among non-Bene Israel.

Some 500 Bene Israel children attend the communal school. (The fact that comparatively few Bene Israel send their children to the communal school is an indication of the low esteem in which the school is held nowadays.) But the majority of Bene Israel children receive their schooling beyond communal boundaries: they attend the Baghdadi school, the municipal schools, and the schools of the Christian missions in India.

A few Bene Israel consult doctors who are also co-members. But as the twenty-five Bene Israel doctors in Bombay[17] are either in general practice some distance from the communal neighbour-hood or expensive specialists, most Bene Israel consult non-Bene Israel doctors or attend the local hospitals. Occasionally, however, the poor of the community ask for and receive free medical advice from Bene Israel specialists—some of whom are noted for their outstanding ability. 'But in any case,' informants relate, 'our Bene Israel specialists always give of their time and skill to the poor of all Indian communities. For they are good people and don't distinguish between members of their own community and others.' Some Bene Israel, however, hold that they are somewhat more entitled to the sympathy and free advice of these famous Bene Israel specialists than members of other communities.

A few Bene Israel consult lawyers who are also co-members. 'There are as many Bene Israel lawyers as there are Bene Israel doctors,' informants relate, 'but some of those in need of legal advice fear that their affairs will become known in the community if they consult Bene Israel lawyers; and so they prefer to ask legal advice of lawyers from other communities.'[18] Needless to say, Bene Israel lawyers insist that such fears are utterly groundless.

Some of the eleven hundred members of the Bene Israel Co-operative Banking Society—established in 1918—are granted loans from time to time. However, there are complaints about the difficulty of obtaining loans from the Society,[19] and I was told that many Bene Israel prefer to borrow from non-communal sources.

While poor by Western standards, as poverty goes in India Bene Israel must be regarded as moderately well off. The community numbers hardly any beggars on the streets or inmates in beggar homes. During the last forty years the community has produced a chief justice of a high court, a president of the Medical Council of India, a mayor of Bombay, a superintendent of one of the largest hospitals for women in India, a State director of public health, a commandant of the Military Academy, and several officers in highly responsible Government positions.

Thus Louis Rabinowitz's report in 1952 that there are but three or four comparatively wealthy Bene Israel 'the rest are as poor as church mice'[20] and Taya Zinkin's description of the Bene Israel in 1960 as 'the world's poorest Jews'[21] are certainly inaccurate. But however inaccurate these impressions, they deserve attention: for they indicate that the successful Bene Israel tend to isolate themselves from, or at least reduce to a minimum, contact with the mainstream of communal life. It is mainly the clerks, that is, the poorer element, who represent the Bene Israel to the world beyond communal boundaries and who are in charge of the organized life within communal boundaries.

It is now time to turn to the habitual goings-on within communal boundaries, the activities through which the community keeps itself intact.

NOTES

1. I was present at two 'Redemption of the First-born Son' ceremonies; at each the priest received some Rs10 (about 15s which is the sum he receives in England; the redemption money mentioned in Numbers, 18:16, is five shekel). I was under the impression that the Baghdadi priest performing the ceremony was not too happy at my presence—perhaps he did not tell his own community that he performed this ceremony for Bene Israel and feared that I might talk about it. Certainly, he told me, 'These people are only liberals in religion; still, I oblige them and do it for them. I consider it a good deed—and what can be wrong about a good deed?'
2. Kehimkar, ibid. pp. 125–6. *Cohen* is the Hebrew word for priest.
3. I had no opportunity to verify this statement. On the other hand, members of the synagogue with which I was mainly associated told me that lately a Baghdadi priest had been attending their services who not only pronounced the 'Blessing of the Priest' free of charge but also donated some money to the synagogue. I met this priest—and as I suspected, found that he is not a Baghdadi proper but a member of the small group of Jews from Afghanistan. He told me, 'I live next-door to Bene Israel and they asked me to come along. I like the service, so I come occasionally. And I make a donation to their synagogue fund because I am broad-minded. Jews from Afghanistan are more broad-minded than those from Baghdad.' He admitted that Jews from Afghanistan are shown more respect by Bene Israel than by Baghdadis 'and it is very nice to be treated with respect'. But he made it very clear that being broad-minded did not include willingness to enter into marriages with Bene Israel. (As has been stated in the Introduction, p. 6, small groups from Aden, Afghanistan, and Iran, form part of the Baghdadi community. But the Jews from Afghanistan seem to have retained their social identity within the Baghdadi community to a much greater extent than those from Aden and Iran. But then, the Jews from Afghanistan are comparative newcomers and, moreover, somewhat less westernized than the Baghdadis proper. However, the great majority of Bene Israel do not distinguish between the various groups that comprise the Baghdadi community.)

4. Thus Lloyd Cabot Briggs and Norina Lami Guéde in their *No More For Ever: A Saharan Jewish Town*, Cambridge, Mass., 1964, p. 26, relate that there were no priests in the Mzab. (The authors are to be congratulated on simply reporting the priestless state of the community without commenting upon its 'uniqueness' or drawing some quite unwarranted conclusions from it—as is done by so many others encountering Jewish communities without priests in their midst.) In his *A Treasury of Jewish Folklore*, New York, 1948, N. Asubel quotes, p. 545, from F. W. Halle 'The Caucasian Mountain Jews', *Commentary*, New York, 1946, that there are no priests or Levites among that group. David G. Mandelbaum in his 'The Jewish Way of Life in Cochin', *Jewish Social Studies*, New York, October 1939, p. 437, writes that the priests of the White Jews of Cochin were becoming extinct, hence the community had to persuade a priest from Baghdad to settle in Cochin. On the other hand, Mandelbaum argues that the absence of priests among the Black Jews of Cochin tends to confirm the possibility that they were originally converts for converted natives could naturally not occupy these hereditary offices. But if the priests among the White Jews could become extinct, could not the same have happened among the Black Jews?

5. I have already referred to this letter on p. 45.

6. Kehimkar, ibid. p. 239.

7. Bene Israel parents constantly begged me to plead their children's case for admission with influential Baghdadis of my acquaintance. But I am told that since so many Baghdadis have now left India, it is much easier for Bene Israel to gain admission to the Baghdadi school.

8. During my stay in Bombay 77 of the 390 children at the Baghdadi school were Bene Israel.

9. There are two Baghdadi places of worship in Bombay, one in the communal neighbourhood, the other in Fort, just north of Colaba. Bene Israel but rarely visit the Baghdadi synagogue in Fort. On one occasion when I encountered members of one of the Bene Israel families attending a Baghdadi wedding in the Fort synagogue, the head of the family told me, 'I am in charge of the department in which the bridegroom works—which is why you see me here!' The few Bene Israel who occasionally worship in a Baghdadi synagogue attend the one in the communal neighbourhood. I know of two Bene Israel who attend the Baghdadi synagogue fairly frequently. One of them likes to attend services daily, and as he lives next-door to the Baghdadi synagogue he sometimes finds it more convenient to worship there than walk to the Bene Israel synagogue some distance from his home. The other used to be president of one of the Bene Israel places of worship, but he quarrelled with his committee and resigned; wishing to avoid the place of worship in which he had once been president, he took to attending the Baghdadi synagogue close to his home. (He is an old man and would find it rather difficult to walk to another Bene Israel synagogue some distance from his home.) Two Bene Israel women attend the Baghdadi synagogue fairly frequently. An informant told me, 'They will say to you that they go there because it is next-door to where they live, but that is not the reason. For many years the Baghdadis have told us that they are better Jews than we are, better in every way. And I suspect that a few of our Bene Israel have taken it to heart, but only a few! And these two women think so much of themselves that they want to go to a better

place of worship. What to do? It is a very complicated problem—as you must have noticed. Of course what I tell you is just my opinion of the matter. They will deny it if you ask them. And only the Lord knows the truth of the human heart. But this is what I think.'

10. I am told that there was once a butcher-shop run by Bene Israel but it has long since closed down.

11. One of these Baghdadis is a well-known journalist. (A number of Baghdadis frequently told me of his professional success with great pleasure. But when referring to his marriage, they pointed out that he was not really a Baghdadi proper but hailed from Aden.) I did not come across further 'intermarriages' in Bombay. However, two Bombay Bene Israel told me that they had considered themselves engaged to Baghdadi girls, but the parents of the girls had prevented the marriages. (One Baghdadi told me that he had considered himself engaged to a girl of the Bene Israel community, but the girl's parents had stopped the marriage. Bene Israel, however, said that this was quite untrue and he had only made up this tale on the spur of the moment because he was going to London and thought that 'you, being so broad-minded, would like the tale and would write him lots of introductions to your friends in London'.

12. That is, the interests of the Black Jews of Cochin centre upon Israel; the interests of the White Jews (who number about 90, many of whom are too old to think of migration) centre upon Canada and Australia.

13. However, many Bene Israel complained that migration to Israel was much easier for Baghdadis than for members of their community.

14. Again, many Bene Israel complained that their representatives are invited only to some of the official functions, while the representatives of the Baghdadi community 'are invited much more often and become personal friends of the people in the Consulate; our people are invited only to a few functions—to give an appearance of broad-mindedness'.

15. The late president of the oldest Bene Israel synagogue told me that on one occasion the Governor of Bombay invited the presidents of the various Bene Israel places of worship to a party. 'I was very pleased. But I was also very surprised. Because the people in the Government interest themselves only in associations which can eventually be made inter-communal. But synagogues cannot be made inter-communal! It was all very surprising. But the Governor died before the party could take place, and succeeding Governors did not repeat the invitation.'

16. An informant said, 'I tell you what I think is the reason for excluding non-Jews—even if they are our best friends—from the synagogue services. When a woman menstruates she should not come to the synagogue. Our Bene Israel women know this—but how can we tell this to others? It would be too embarrassing. And how can we say that men can come but not the women? It is very embarrassing, so we say to all that they cannot come to the synagogue services. But perhaps other Bene Israel will not tell this. Probably they will be too embarrassed to tell this. But I think that this is the true reason for excluding non-Jews from the synagogue services.'

17. There are Bene Israel doctors in private practice in Poona; a few hold hospital appointments in various parts of the country.

18. In any case, as few Bene Israel lawyers have gained the same professional fame as some of the Bene Israel doctors, many members of the community do not consider that advice from Bene Israel lawyers is necessarily the best that can be obtained.

19. But a member of the Society's committee told me. 'No doubt some people will have told you that we are unfair about granting loans. But we aren't unfair—only careful! And we are not ashamed of it. On the contrary, we boasted about it in the Annual Report.' (The Report states, 'The Managing Committee was very particular about granting loans.')

20. Rabinowitz, ibid. p. 69.

21. Taya Zinkin, 'The World's Poorest Jews', *Guardian*, Manchester, April 13, 1960.

Part III

WITHIN COMMUNAL
BOUNDARIES

G

7
Marriage and the Family

Kehimkar enumerates some of the customs introduced among the Bene Israel in imitation of local usages:

Fixing an auspicious day for marriage; calling out five un-widowed or unmarried women, as is done on every auspicious occasion; putting on bangles on the wrist of the bride a day previous to her marriage; waving copper or silver coin round the bride and bridegroom (not to avert evil, like the Hindus, for the latter throw the same afterwards to people of the lower castes in order that evil may be averted from the pair and be transferred to these low people, whilst among the Bene Israel, the pieces are presented to the very sisters of the bride and bridegroom); throwing rice on their bodies as a sign of fertility; rubbing their hands and feet with Mendi (Henna); fastening together the hems of their handkerchiefs as a symbol of union; the tying of a necklace (Lacha) of glass and golden beads round the neck of the bride at the conclusion of the marriage ceremony; making the newly married pair tear out rolls of leaves, held between the teeth, from the mouth of each other; making them play the games of odd and even; the bride-groom's going away from the bride in pretended ill humour; the hiding by the bridegroom of a betelnut or some ornament which is to be searched for and found by the bride; the breaking of the bangles and of the Lacha, worn by a woman, after the death of her husband; and the discontinuing of the use of the nose ring by a widow. Though the introduction of these local customs is to be ascribed to our ancestors, it must be borne in mind that time and circumstances must have compelled them to practise them. We are, however, glad to find that most of the local customs named have gradually been given up by our people during the last fifty or sixty years; and the rest are also on the eve of extinction.[1]

But in this respect Bene Israel hardly differ from Jews elsewhere who also have adopted some of the customs of the host society. Marriage proper, however, is performed according to the traditional religious rites—'according to the Law of Moses and Israel': the ancient phrase used in the marriage service which expresses the resolve of the bridegroom and bride to lead their common life according to the rule and manner of Judaism.

This chapter, then, should provide some comment on the recent storm which raged over the acceptability of Bene Israel for purposes of marriage.

ARRANGING A MARRIAGE

Bene Israel are very much immersed in the present. Thus however hospitable and helpful, however intrigued by my interest in their memories of the old standards of life, only a few were able to provide much information about what they once had and did. Moreover, I was continually struck not only by how little they seem to remember about the 'old ways' but also by the absence of nostalgia for the past.

There is, however, an exception to this tendency to concentrate on the present, to live 'modern-wise'—marriage is still primarily arranged in the traditional way, that is, by the parents. Nor is this surprising: Bene Israel marry young—as soon as the boy has stepped into a job and there is enough money to pay for the expenses of the wedding ceremonies, his parents will try to find a bride for him; but in any case, the restraint which characterizes the relations between those of opposite sex makes it exceedingly difficult to conduct a courtship.

Kehimkar writes:

> The bitter experience of the evils that arise from the institution of early marriages, combined with the growing knowledge of their scriptures, have taught the Bene Israel to almost give up this pernicious institution. . . . No marriage as a rule now-a-days takes place unless the bridegroom is a youngman (*sic*) of twenty or twenty-one years old, and the bride be 14 or 15. . . . As soon as the intention of getting their son married is formed by the parents, their first care is to see whether the family with which they would like to connect themselves is of pure Hebrew blood. They then ascertain if the members of that family suffer from any hereditary disease. When they have ascertained after a

searching inquiry that the family is of pure blood and has no natural defects, they decide upon the union tentatively, and ask the boy whether he likes the proposal; but should he not like it, they proceed to find out another suitable bride for him. When parents have at last obtained their son's consent, they send match-makers to the parents of the girl to know whether they would accept their proposal. . . . The parents of the girl institute inquiries similar to those done by the parents of the boy, and in addition to this they inquire whether the boy be an intelligent and promising young man, and whether he bears a good character, and can earn his livelihood. According to the information thus gained they either refuse or accept the proposal. . . . If the parents of the boy and the girl have agreed, the matrimonial union is brought about and the parents of the boy go to the girl's house and present a small quantity of sugar. After a day or two the ceremony of Espousal is performed, when relatives of the boy and the girl are invited.[2]

Kehimkar wrote in the late nineteenth century. However, one wonders whether early marriages were really as rare in the late nineteenth century as Kehimkar suggests. An informant writes: 'While my father was still a student he was pressed to marry. My eldest uncle had married when he was only fifteen, and my second uncle when he was barely eighteen. My father graduated at the end of 1884 and at the end of 1885 he was married. As, in the meantime, girls more suited to his age of twenty-two were already married off, he had to marry a girl of nine. My eldest sister was born in 1889 (when her mother was only thirteen or fourteen) and in March 1892 her mother died in childbirth at an age when today girls are just out of school. My father married for the second time in March 1893. My mother was then fifteen years of age— a very advanced age for a girl to remain unmarried in those days. Perhaps it was because of her advanced age that she had to be content with a widower!' (However this informant admits that 'nine was somewhat exceptionally low even for 1885.')

Contemporary marriage negotiations are very similar to those described by Kehimkar in the late nineteenth century. Nowadays however, the prospective bride and groom will be somewhat older —the girl will be in her late teens and the boy in his early twenties; the educational attainments of the prospective bride and groom will again be carefully considered.

Cross-cousin marriage, that is, marriage between cousins

related through parents who are siblings of different sexes, is permitted but does not appear to be a very common form nowadays. Still, a woman informant in her sixties told me that in olden times cross-cousin marriage was regarded as the ideal marriage type. Others, however, said, 'That one is so old-fashioned, she clings to customs that nobody has even heard about. Perhaps it was so in *her* family and she thinks it was the general custom.' Another informant writes that cross-cousin marriage was very common in families like his with records of military service. 'In the past marriages were sometimes settled while the parties were in the cradle. Now mothers dare not make such compacts as they are liable to be repudiated by the men (and at times the women) concerned.' A man in his eighties insisted that although some did indeed marry their cross-cousins, 'people with spirit did not! If you marry kinsfolk you remain stuck in the same old circle. It was held best to marry into new circles— thereby making new friends who may turn out to be interesting and useful!' But as Bene Israel form a comparatively small group and in the 1880s, the period my informant was talking about, numbered only 7,000, even 'people with spirit' would have found it hard to marry into completely new circles.

Proposals originate with the parents of the boy. However, an informant told me that in a family of many girls their parents may take the initiative and in a very covert manner suggest to the parents of suitable young men that they are prepared to consider offers for their daughters; I have no reason to doubt this informant who also told me that as I was getting to know 'the innermost affairs of members of the community', I was in an excellent position to suggest a suitable match for her daughter— 'and why should not all this information you are collecting serve some useful purpose?' However, except among the comparatively small number of professional Bene Israel, the difficulty is not finding a suitable match but avoiding the quarrels that tend to arise between the engagement and the wedding. Informants say, 'Although our Bene Israel have no dowry system, the cost of the wedding is considerable and balancing it fairly is not easy.' Indeed, quarrelling between the engagement and the wedding is so common that those who manage to avoid it will relate again and again that 'everything was settled peacefully and in a friendly manner'.

'LOVE' MARRIAGE

Although marriage is arranged primarily by the parents, it is hoped that the couple will come to love each other. Thus a young member of the community spending a year in London whose parents had informed him by letter that they were arranging a match for him, wrote to me:

> . . . about my marriage, I have to inform you that I am not engaged yet, as it is the custom with the Bene Israel to get the couple married as early as possible, once the engagement has taken place. Time limit varies from family to family, and with my family it is customary to get the son or daughter married within six to nine months after the engagement. Of course the marriage is postponed for a year if the kin of the bride or bridegroom is dead after the engagement period. The girl I am getting married to is my cousin and it is an approved marriage by both the parties and it is going to be a love-marriage also. . . .

Occasionally, however, two young people who have met at school or at some function and have managed to talk to one another alone and come to like each other will ask their parents to negotiate the marriage in the traditional manner. Again, a few 'love' matches proper have occurred, that is, the young people had come to like each other and did not ask their parents to negotiate the match in the traditional manner but simply informed them that they wished to get married. Although the public behaviour of couples who have entered into or are about to enter into 'love' matches proper is just as restrained as that between those whose matches have been arranged in the traditional manner, people know just how the match has come about.

There are instances of parents successfully objecting to 'love' matches. But if the two sets of parents approve of the choice, they will not oppose the match just because it has not been arranged in the traditional manner. For parents want their children to be happily married. Besides, once the parents have been told that their children love each other, and there is no objection to the match, there is a strong obligation to avoid quarrelling over the wedding arrangements and therefore a good chance to cut down on the cost of the wedding without running the risk that it will break off the match. On the other hand, there is an important objection to 'love' marriages proper—for if love comes to be considered as an essential before entering into marriage, and courting is to be allowed, how then is intermarriage to be avoided?

MARRIAGES BETWEEN GORA AND KALA BENE ISRAEL

Marriages between Gora and Kala Bene Israel are the result of 'falling in love' and are likely to increase. An informant writes, 'Today Kala are not subjected to any discrimination, except perhaps that there is a reluctance to marry among them. But even I who have so few contacts know of two marriages—one celebrated in January last—between Gora and Kala Bene Israel and no one dares to argue that such marriages are irregular from the religious point of view. In another generation the distinction should have disappeared.'

He adds, 'It is not quite fair to us to say that it serves us right to be branded as half Jews in Israel because we branded a section of our own community as Kala in India. Whatever we did in the past we are rectifying. In Israel barriers are being given legal sanction and thus perpetuated.'

MARRIAGES BETWEEN BENE ISRAEL AND BAGHDADIS

Like marriages between Gora and Kala Bene Israel, marriages between Bene Israel and Baghdadis are the result of 'falling in love'; but such marriages are rare.

In a recent communication an informant writes, 'My impression is that there are not as many Bene Israel–Baghdadi marriages as there used to be, perhaps because Bene Israel men no longer feel that they are getting a bargain in a Baghdadi girl. Baghdadi men seldom married Bene Israel girls.' Though I only encountered two Bombay Bene Israel who had married Baghdadi girls and two Bombay Baghdadis who had married Bene Israel girls, I know of marriages between Bene Israel and Baghdadi girls in Calcutta and Delhi.

INTERMARRIAGE

There is a definite and deep disdain for intermarriage. It is in fact so recent an innovation that Kehimkar, writing in the late nineteenth century, could ask rhetorically whether there was 'a single instance in which marriage has been known to take place with a heathenish woman'.[3] Bene Israel say that they have a 'double reason' for eschewing intermarriage—'it was frowned upon by Judaism and it is rigidly prohibited by all castes'. Indeed, every single instance of intermarriage provokes such prolonged comment and vigorous disapproval that it must take considerable courage to embark upon it; nor is disapproval tempered by such factors as the high-caste Hindu descent or European origin of the non-Jewish partner.

I know of four Bene Israel men who have married European non-Jewesses—two married Scottish girls, one married an English girl while studying in London, another, a clerk, married a French schoolteacher working in Bombay. Of these four only one expressed the hope that intermarriage would one day become common in India 'so that the country's two great curses, religion and caste, could come to an end'. In his youth this man had been involved in communal affairs, but later he devoted himself mainly to professional and political activities, becoming exceedingly well known and highly esteemed in both fields. I met him shortly before his death when he told me of his fear that in spite of all his efforts it would take a very long time before intermarriage would become increasingly frequent. But his case was somewhat unusual: for even those members of the community who have done well professionally and are involved in Indian rather than communal affairs indicate a strong preference for marrying within the community.

From the point of view of Judaism, while the children of a Jewish father and a non-Jewish (that is, non-converted) mother are not Jewish, the children of a Jewish mother and a non-Jewish (that is, non-converted) father are Jewish. It is true that in practice the children of a Jewish mother and a non-Jewish father may be brought up in the father's group—but the ruling is important in cases in which the children of a mixed union wish to be treated as Jews: if their mother is Jewish, they will have to be accepted into the religious fold of Jewry; if the father only is Jewish, they will have to be converted.[4] (And from the point of view of Judaism a person who is converted in accordance with Jewish rites is regarded as a Jew.)

Men seem to marry out more than women—but, then, the men

of the community enjoy greater social freedom than the women and thus have more opportunities to meet outsiders.[5] Moreover, once the opposition to the marriage has abated a little, men find it easier than women to bring a non-Jewish partner into the communal fold—it is easier for a woman to become converted than for a man (who would have to undergo circumcision); again, men play a much bigger part than women in the affairs of the community, especially in the affairs of the synagogue, so that male converts would find it much more difficult than female converts to participate in communal affairs. Thus non-Jewesses marrying Bene Israel tend to become converted to Judaism—I use the word 'tend' intentionally: non-Jewesses marrying Bene Israel are not always converted to Judaism—there is a religious marriage, and the children will be brought up in the Jewish faith. I heard of only one Indian non-Jew who had become converted to Judaism in one of the Bene Israel places of worship; after his conversion his engagement to a girl of the Bene Israel community was announced, and the couple was planning a synagogue wedding. (Two such conversions are said to have occurred in a Baghdadi place of worship; these two men then married Baghdadi girls.)

The registry office was the setting for the few marriages that have occurred between Bene Israel girls and non-Jews—and although these girls have kept in touch with their parents and siblings, it is exceedingly unlikely that their children will be brought up in the Jewish faith.

It has been pointed out that intermarriage takes courage. As more and more members of the community plan emigration to Israel, it is likely to take even more courage: as some put it, 'We have enough difficulties convincing the Israelis that we are pure Jews—so can you imagine what it would be like if upon our arrival there they would find out that some of the wives were recent converts?'[6]

POLYGYNY

Polygyny, marriage between one man and more than one woman, is not part of the traditional Jewish way of life: in latter biblical days polygyny seems to have been rare among the ordinary people; of the rabbis of the Talmud none is known to have practised polygyny. In the West monogamy became more and more the general rule so that in the 11th century Rabbenu Gershom of Mayence: 'the Light of the Exile', famous as the author of a series of regulations intended to adapt Jewish life to the conditions which it had to face in Europe, found little opposition when he instituted a ban against polygynists. This ban was generally accepted by all Ashkenazim.[7]

Polygyny among the Bene Israel is nowadays exceedingly rare: I encountered fewer than a dozen cases in Bombay, Poona and the Konkan. In Bombay there was only one case in which the husband and his two wives shared the same home. But in this case the second wife is so much younger than her co-wife (and, moreover, of an unusually docile disposition) that she appears to be a daughter rather than a co-wife; both wives are childless. Again, in the Konkan I encountered a three-generation household in which the senior male and his son had each married two wives; and it was said that the married grandson in a bout of fury had threatened his wife that he too intended to take a second wife.

A man may marry a second wife if the first one has no offspring or no male offspring. Thus a polygynist living in Bombay told me that his first wife had had seven daughters before giving birth to a son. He very much wanted another son but feared that 'it would take seven more daughters before the first wife had another son' so he took a second wife. However, the second wife had only daughters—while the only son by his first wife died. He took this to be a heavenly punishment 'for upsetting the first wife by taking a second' and now wished to migrate to Israel, with his two wives and ten daughters, there to atone for his sin. Another polygynist told me that he had married a second wife because he needed someone to look after his field in the Konkan. 'If I employ someone—will he do it properly? A wife will do it properly! So the second wife lives there with her children and I visit her there. But the rest of the time I spend in Bombay with my first wife and her children. It is a very good arrangement!' He added that in former times a man could live with his two wives as one family under one roof—something which is recognized to be almost impossible nowadays. Kehimkar, however, implies that even in former times co-wives did not always succeed in living together under one roof as one family:

If a man obtains no issue by his first marriage, he commonly married a second time, but some people re-marry without any cause. Provision for the maintenance and clothing etc. of the first wife is made whenever a Bene Israel marries a second one. The first wife is provided with an income every month of from Rs 5 to Rs 25 or 30 according to the circumstances of the man, if both wives do not live harmoniously with each other. Besides the maintenance money, the first wife gets a couple of bodices, two or four saries, bed sheets, mantles, etc. This custom has prevailed among the Bene Israel from very ancient times, and is analogous to the rule laid down in the Mishna Ketuboth viii, 8.[8]

Many Bene Israel wondered whether nowadays a man can have two legal wives. Some thought it was illegal, and that those performing the religious ceremony which legitimizes the marriage 'would get into trouble if it came out'. Others held that it was legal for members of the minorities to marry more than one wife —provided that it was in consonance with the religious rules of the minority and that the first wife was childless or had at least given her consent. However, most informants held that it was not worth while to inquire into the legal position—'The whole business of marrying two wives is so rare and is getting rarer still; besides, it might be a bad move to inquire: people could begin to think that polygamy is common among our Bene Israel! Better to keep quiet about it!'[9]

But in any case, polygyny is neither cheap nor prestigeful; it is something 'unfit for educated, sensitive people'. Moreover, kinsmen of the polygynist tend to be ashamed of him. Thus on one occasion one of the oldest and most orthodox members of the community told me that his brother was no longer orthodox— which caused him great sorrow. As soon as he left, the others present informed me that the brother was not only unorthodox but also a polygnyist—'You may be sure that that causes him even greater sorrow, so much that he couldn't tell you about it. We only mention it because it must be of great scientific interest to you!' It is recognized that nowadays orthodoxy is a matter of choice. 'Top People' among the Bene Israel—that is, the educated element—may be orthodox or not (usually not), but they are most unlikely to be polygynists. In other words, adherence to the traditional Jewish way of life is a matter of choice, adherence to the Western way of life is prestigeful. And Bene Israel are not slow to recognize that those with most contacts among their European co-religionists are the educated, usually non-orthodox members of the community.

DIVORCE AND WIDOW RE-MARRIAGE

Deuteronomy 23:2, states 'A bastard shall not enter into the assembly of the Lord; even to the tenth generation shall none of his enter into the assembly of the Lord.' However, a bastard does not mean a child born out of wedlock, but the child of an adulterous or incestuous union—for example, the child of a woman whose previous marriage had not been ended according to Jewish law. Again, tenth generation implies never. (The numeral 'ten' denotes an indefinitely large number.)

The recent controversy which raged over the acceptability of Bene Israel as 'pure' Jews for purposes of marriage with members of other communities of Jews was based on the suspicion that during their long isolation from the mainstream of Jewish life they had been ignorant of the Jewish law relating to divorce and the levirate and that, therefore, according to the rule laid down in Deuteronomy 23:2, they were debarred from entering into 'the assembly of the Lord', that is, from entering into marriage with co-religionists from other communities.

According to Jewish law a couple can be divorced only if the husband writes (or causes to be written) a Bill of Divorce, *get*, which he hands to his wife, saying, 'This is thy *get*, thou art divorced and art permitted to marry whomsoever thou wilt.' Again, according to Deuteronomy 25:5–10, if a man dies and leaves no children one of his brothers—according to seniority— should marry the widow. 'And it shall be that the first-born that she bearest shall succeed in the name of his brother that is dead, that his name not be blotted out of Israel.' If the brothers refuse to marry the widow the eldest brother, upon whom the duty lies first, is to be put to shame publicly by the act of *chalizah*, that is, after he has confirmed before a court that he declines to marry the widow, the latter takes off his right shoe and spits on the floor while proclaiming 'Thus should be done to the man who does not build the house of his brother.' After the *chalizah* the widow is allowed to marry whomever she likes. In Talmudical times the view already prevailed that *chalizah* was to be preferred to the levirate marriage, because the latter was not always performed from religious motives. Nowadays the levirate marriage has passed out of use, and only *chalizah* is practised. No plan acceptable to Orthodox authorities has been found which would make *chalizah* unnecessary.

As suggested previously, there is reason to believe that the Bene Israel were never as isolated from Jewry nor as ignorant of Judaism as their historical memories imply. Obviously however, one does not know whether they were ignorant of the Jewish law relating to divorce and levirate. On the other hand, their knowledge or ignorance of Jewish law relating to divorce and levirate is immaterial since 'Bene Israel women feel it to be very immodest to live with another husband after they have once been married. . . . When a husband and wife do not agree with each other, the husband does not give a bill of divorce to the wife except in the case of adultery, nor does a woman seek to obtain a divorce, and she cannot re-marry.'[10] Again, it has been pointed out that widow re-marriage was frowned upon.[11] The childless widow would be taken in by a kinsman. True, Bene Israel admit that a widow with children might find it difficult to be taken in by a kinsman and she might consider re-marriage—but only after the greatest amount of persuasion; but then, the levirate is only concerned with childless widows. It seems therefore that had more been known about the Bene Israel—that is, had it been known that the Bene Israel did not practise divorce until they overcame their antipathy to it and learnt the Jewish forms from the Cochin and Baghdadi Jews, and that they frowned upon widow re-marriage, probably in imitation of the practice of the higher Hindu castes—the storm which raged over their acceptability for purposes of marriage need never have arisen.

Nowadays divorce does occur, though it is still rather rare. Rarer still is widow re-marriage—as inimical to the Bene Israel as it is to the Hindus.

THE TRADITIONAL JOINT HOUSEHOLD

As among other Indian groups, traditionally the joint household is the proper form of family organization. Sons bring their wives to their father's dwelling. The father manages finances, directs affairs, and settles disputes between members of the household. The wives of the sons help with the housework which is organized and directed by their mother-in-law. At the death of the parents the sons may continue to live together on much the same terms, the eldest son taking the place of the father; otherwise the group may dissolve, eventually forming a series of new joint households.

Nowadays, however, the traditional joint household is very much the exception. True, it is not unusual for *one* married son to remain with his parents. What is unusual is for *all* married sons to remain with their parents and to put all their earnings into a common pool. I did in fact come across three such traditional joint households in Bombay—but in each of these three cases there were only two sons; in each case the sons worked in the same office and there was very little difference in the incomes they earned; moreover, in each case accommodation was less cramped than usual, allowing each couple some privacy. Again, although in each case those concerned stressed that they were only doing 'the proper thing', nevertheless they expressed great satisfaction at having succeeded where so many others had failed.

TENSIONS IN THE JOINT HOUSEHOLD

Relationships within the joint household are rarely completely free and easy. Tensions may develop chiefly between mother-in-law and daughter-in-law, between father and sons, between brothers. But whereas tensions between mother-in-law and daughter-in-law are regrettable, tensions between father and son and between brothers are held to be morally reprehensible. Certainly Bene Israel prefer to put the blame for misunderstandings and conflicts within the joint household upon the mother-in-law/daughter-in-law relationship—traditionally a difficult and even harsh one. 'There may be quarrels about the division of labour in the household. Often the daughter-in-law thinks she is being worked too hard. It stands to reason that this will lead to quarrelling and persuading the husband to secure separate accommodation.' And as nowadays the daughter-in-law will be at least in her late teens and, moreover, is likely to have had a much better education than her mother-in-law, she tends to resent her subordinate position. Again, nowadays many young wives like to romanticize their marriage: 'In the evening the young wife may ask her husband to take her for a walk or even to the pictures while the mother-in-law thinks it is just a waste of time and she would be better employed doing more of the housework—so there will be quarrels again. Older people among our Bene Israel community don't always understand about romance.'

Still, it is admitted that, especially nowadays, living in a joint household may be as great a strain on the young husband as on his wife: he too marries at a later age than previously; he too is likely to have had a better education than his father; just as the young woman wants a greater voice in the management of the household so the young man wants a greater voice in the management of the finances. If he is ambitious and holds a lucrative post, he may wish to save some of his income for his children's education rather than put it into a common pool to help finance the education of a younger brother or contribute to the maintenance of a less ambitious or less lucky member of the household. On the other hand, those with a lower income to contribute may feel looked down upon or even discriminated against and decide that the economic advantages which accrue from living in a joint household are more than offset by the tensions which it entails.

To prevent or resolve tensions, the father may ask his sons to contribute merely the cost of their board, and that of their wives and children, to the joint household budget, allowing them to bank the rest of their earnings in their own name. 'In this way,' informants said, 'because it is so much cheaper than setting up a separate home, the father provides a cheap boarding-house; and in this way he may succeed in keeping his sons under his roof— for a while.' But sooner or later there will be crises—one son may be temporarily unable to carry out his obligations, another will aspire to a higher standard of living, there will be invidious comparisons, jealousy and quarrels—forcing the joint household apart.

Bene Israel are not given to eulogizing the joint household of former times—fathers could be harsh towards their sons and mothers-in-law could be cruel towards their daughters-in-law. Nevertheless, informants said, 'families remained together because it was the proper way of life; perhaps sons were less sophisticated in their wants in those days, but they knew their duty and did it too!' But they also married then at an earlier age —at which it would have been difficult to escape parental control.

Besides, if sons 'knew their duty and did it too', it would appear that they did it in homes somewhat larger than those of today—usually one room in a large, overcrowded, insanitary building—allowing each couple some privacy. For Kehimkar describes the homes of the Bene Israel in Bombay, Poona and Thana, as consisting of sleeping rooms, a general sitting room, a veranda and a kitchen. (Some owned the houses in which they lived, others lived in rented houses.) Moreover, it would seem that in those days the father, though harsh, was usually able to provide for his sons—some of whom would squander their patrimony in speculation and extravagance in a short time, something for which Bene Israel no longer have the means or the inclination.

Thus Kehimkar quotes an account published by the Rev. J. H. Lord in the *Bombay Diocesan Record* (which also appeared in the *Bombay Gazette*, 31 January, 1885): 'The Bene Israel community possess their own peculiar faults of internal dissension, and of a growing tendency on the part of their rising generation to extravagance, squandering of property, and intemperance, yet this again co-existing with a laudable desire on the part of the leaders of their community to rise out of the decay of centuries, and make their synagogue services reasonable, worthy and devout (according to their knowledge) and to educate their children.'[12]

Again, while in former times it would have been exceedingly difficult for a son to set up a separate household, there was a way in which the pent-up tensions could be honourably relieved, namely by enlisting in the regiments of the East India Company. The following account, one of a number cited in Kehimkar's book, shows something of the strain which not infrequently characterized the relations between the father and his married sons in the traditional joint household:

Robenji Isaji Nawgaonkar, i.e. Reuben son of Isaac of the village of Nawgaon, was born in Bombay in the thirties of the 19th century. The original home of the family, like that of all Bene-Israelites, was in the Colaba district of the Konkan, the western coast of India. Here they were oil-pressers and agriculturists. When the family left the Konkan and came to Bombay is not known. It must have been in the days when Bombay was beginning to be built up and settled in, for Isaac is known to have been a building contractor. Reuben learnt to read and write both Marathi and English. . . . He was the eldest son in

H

the family, was fair-complexioned and tall, and was of a gentle and affectionate nature. He was married early, but seems to have remained at home not doing anything in particular. Perhaps as the father was doing well, the sons were in no particular hurry to begin to earn a living for themselves. The father Isaac, however, was a stern old man, tyrannical in his ways and would spare neither wife nor grown up sons and daughters-in-law in his bouts of fury. Reuben was now a married man with children. His sensitive nature could not stand his father's ungovernable temper any longer. He quietly left home one day and enlisted in one of the British Indian Regiments stationed then in Bombay. In those days there were very few recruits knowing how to read and write, and Reuben with his knowledge of Marathi and English and a working knowledge of Urdu, was welcomed.[13]

Indeed, many Bene Israel left their homes in the wake of the army and some took part in expeditions abroad—though it is not suggested that all Bene Israel who joined the army did so in order to escape harsh heads of the joint household.

TYPES OF CONTEMPORARY HOUSEHOLDS

Of the ninety-four households studied in Bombay only three were of the traditional joint household type,[14] fifty-one were of the contemporary joint household type, and forty were elementary households.[15]

Nowadays married sons may stay on in the parental home for a short time—either until the first child is born or another brother marries; and the last son to marry may remain with his father. Indeed, nowadays the father may take the initiative in securing separate accommodation for his sons as soon as they marry, keeping only his favourite son with him—the one most likely to support him in his old age or whose wife has the most gentle disposition and will be able and willing to get on with her mother-in-law. On the other hand, informants insisted, 'When the father retires and he or his wife need something especially expensive, all the sons will make a little contribution towards the expense; and sometimes all the sons will make a little contribution all the time. Wherever they live, only very few Bene Israel will forsake their parents—but the son who remains with his parents will have the pleasure of knowing that he is doing the proper thing and people will praise him for it!' Some added, 'At least the other sons will talk him into it—they will point out that someone should remain, and that he will get pleasure and praise because he is doing the right thing.'

Today, then, the most usual type of household consists of a man, his wife, one married son and his wife and children, as well as the unmarried children of the senior couple. Again, sometimes an unmarried or widowed kinsman or kinswoman of the father may join the household. Occasionally the household includes an unmarried or widowed kinsman or kinswoman of the mother. Bene Israel say that the latter may happen if the father is very kind—or if the mother has a very strong personality and insists on it.

The father is the head of this household, in charge of its economy, while his wife organizes the household tasks. But I have heard it said, 'Nobody listens to my father' (a not uncommon explanation for which is 'because he has no money'), and 'My wife is the mistress of the home, my mother just lives with me.' True, such outspokenness is rather rare; and in any case, there are households in which the parents control affairs and exert authority over a married son and his wife and family. Nevertheless, many Bene Israel admit that nowadays the position of the senior couple is determined by personality rather than by tradition.

The great majority of Bene Israel held that, except for the few who are enamoured of tradition or feel incapable of carrying the responsibility of a family by themselves, a young married couple will desire to set up a separate household. A few achieve their desire for a separate household on marriage, most must wait awhile. But informants held that the desire for a separate household is usually so strong that few are deterred for long merely by the higher cost of living which the break-up will involve.

The new household may be in the same building or very near the household of the parents of the husband. Occasionally, however, the young wife will enlist her parents' help in securing separate accommodation, in which case the new household may be in the same building or very near the household of the parents of the wife. Unless there have been conflicts and quarrels, establishing a separate household does not result in any stigma falling on the family nor does it cause gossip in the community.

Bene Israel say that however hurt the parents may feel when their married sons leave them, they realize that it is the trend of the time for the young couple to do what is convenient and enjoyable; some even say that it is well known that better-educated and sensitive people everywhere set up separate households—and that it can only add to the prestige of the Bene Israel community if its members act like better-educated and sensitive people.

Occasionally such an elementary household may be joined for a while by an unmarried sibling of the husband—this may happen at the death of the husband's parents.

Sometimes an unmarried or widowed man or woman will live alone. Those living alone usually follow a profession sufficiently lucrative to allow them to finance their own domestic arrangements. Occasionally unmarried or widowed siblings, again usually only those involved in the professions, may decide to share their domestic arrangements. In theory all the members of such a household are of equal status. But in practice there is much flexibility in such an arrangement, and the senior member or the one who has the greatest professional achievements to his or her credit may be regarded as the head of such a household.

INHERITANCE

Kehimkar writes:

> There has been a custom amongst the Bene Israel from time immemorial that on the death of an intestate Bene Israel all his property should be divided amongst his sons and widow or widows. . . . The expenses of a daughter or daughter's marriage, are borne by the estate. . . . The daughters are not entitled to any moiety. . . .[16]

An informant states:

> H. S. Kehimkar says something about the earlier practices. . . . Even after 1865, when the first civil legislation was passed, where there was no dispute and no danger of resort to courts, I imagine the old custom continued. I know that in 1892 (some time before I was born, however) my father and uncle (two brothers) shared their father's property (pitifully small as it was) without giving anything to their sisters, excepting for some articles of clothing or utensils as mementos. Daughters

were supposed to have been given their shares at the time of marriage. According to law, brothers and sisters should have shared the property equally. The rule is that, if no will exists, the wife (or husband) takes one-third if there are children, and one-half (or a minimum of Rs 5,000) if there are none. The children share equally the remaining two-thirds, and the kindred, blood relations of the nearest degree, that is, parents, brothers and sisters of the deceased, share the other half where there are no children. If a child has died leaving progeny, then that progeny shares the portion which would have gone to the child if he were alive at the time of the death of the parent whose property is inherited. There are detailed provisions for various contingencies—for example, the wife gets all the property if there are no children or near kindred, and the children get the whole property if there is no wife; the property of a person without wife or children goes to his parents and brothers and sisters. I think that among the uneducated, there is still the impression that married daughters get nothing as they are presumed to have got their share at the time of marriage in the form of jewellery, clothes and utensils, and unmarried daughters only get maintenance until they marry. Usually the widow and sons keep whatever property there is, the widow keeping the utensils until she dies and then giving them to her daughters-in-law (or, surreptitiously, to her daughters). As awareness of legal rights spreads, daughters are doubtless asserting their rights, and many people take the precaution of making wills, particularly when sons separate after marriage.

Indeed, most informants held that a man who has had the ability to accumulate a worthwhile estate also has the intelligence to make a will so as to avoid quarrels about the division of his possessions. Asked what was meant by estate, informants said, 'Mainly money and jewellery', but added. 'In most cases there is no estate to worry about.' But whether it is legally justified or even worthwhile, quarrels over inheritance, however pitiful, do occur, giving rise to strained relations between kinsfolk, in particular between siblings.

THE KINSHIP NETWORK

Tradition calls for solidarity between all kin, even those of remote degree, for mutual assistance, social support, and economic help.

But it is a tradition very much in conflict with the contemporary situation: few informants had not experienced the bitterness of having what they considered a rightful claim upon even a close kinsman rejected. For the desire for a higher standard of living and for giving one's children a good education involves never-ending financial burdens that make it difficult to carry out traditional kinship obligations such as helping siblings in distress and, indeed, occasionally result in the neglect of needy parents. But while people continually criticise one another for failure to live up to kinship obligations, they nevertheless realize that harsh modern conditions provide an obstacle to the full discharge of such obligations.

Nowadays, then, it is the ritual occasions in the life of an individual—birth, circumcision, redemption of the first-born son, engagement, marriage, death—that provide the main scope for kinship. Bene Israel relate that these occasions used to be marked by elaborate ritual involving expense far above the income of many of them, but that nowadays the observance of these occasions depends on the piety and wealth of the individual. But whether elaborately celebrated or not, it is on these occasions that kinsfolk—unless they are completely at odds and freely express their enmity—help one another by delivering invitations, helping with the buying, preparing, and serving of food, and so on. This is not to say that friends will not help with the preparations too, but it is on these occasions that kinsfolk will assist one another where and when possible.

Bene Israel were immensely amused at my attempts to discover the kinsfolk involved on these occasions. Informants insisted that there is no difference between matrilineal and patrilineal kinsfolk: the relevant circle varies. For example, it may be that mother's kinsman is better versed in Hebrew than father's kinsman, in which case the former will be asked to preside over a ceremony that requires some knowledge of Hebrew. (On the other hand, a man who is in the habit of reducing his wife to tears over some minor shortcomings during such ceremonies is likely to give prominence to his kin rather than to hers.)

The significance of kinship in other fields is slight. They are not in a position to help one another to find jobs, they rarely work together in the same office, they do not use it as an appeal for gaining support in elections to communal office. Bene Israel say that of course kinsfolk may be friends—'there is no rule that says they can't be'—in which case they are likely to be very close indeed; but unless kinsfolk are friends, 'one can't rely on them'.

The situation that I have just described obtains mainly between the clerks or those in equivalent posts, that is, those most in need of help and least able to give it. It is somewhat different between members of the professional element. Those established in the professions—especially if they are childless or unmarried—may be able to honour kinship obligations much more easily than the clerks—and it is held that they frequently do so. But it is believed that even among the professional Bene Israel the tie of kinship is much more readily acknowledged if it is supported by that of friendship. Again, I have heard it said that the tendency among the professional Bene Israel to help their kin is buttressed by the consideration that one is being helpful to those who will be able to reciprocate one day. On the other hand, some informants considered that this was a most unfair suspicion—'These people are not only kinsfolk, they also respect one another for their many achievements while the clerks have not got such a good opinion of one another; they feel that to help one another is a waste of time and only helping the undeserving.'

THE LANGUAGE OF KINSHIP

English kinship terms tend to be used even by those least familiar with the English language. Many informants held that this was only natural: English has fewer kinship terms than Marathi and Bene Israel nowadays acknowledge fewer kinship ties than had previously been the case. (One informant added amidst general approval and amusement, 'See, you have turned us all into sociologists!')

But kinship terms may also be used to address Bene Israel unrelated by ties of kin: because, as informants explained, in so small a community as the Bene Israel, members should not be real strangers to one another. Older people may be addressed as uncles and aunts, people of one's own generation as brothers and sisters.

Informants insisted, however, that it would be an insult to address those one knows well by kinship terms: within the community the use of kinship terms to address those not related by ties of kin expresses distance rather than intimacy. On the other hand, people of other communities with whom one enjoys a good relationship may be addressed by kinship terms—in which case it expresses both intimacy and respect.

Members of the professional element are addressed by name. This is not a sign of intimacy but, on the contrary, reflects the feeling that these people belong to the nation rather than to the Bene Israel community.

Those among the clerks with whom I was in continual contact used to address me by name—usually 'Miss Schifra', or if they knew me more intimately only by my given name. Others with whom I had less frequent contact sometimes addressed me by a kinship term. On the other hand, members of the small group of Israelis working in Bombay—even those working among the Bene Israel, like the Jewish Agency-subsidized teachers—were addressed by name. Informants remarked that it was very much in the interest of the community to impress upon Israelis that Bene Israel were Westernized—while it was held that I would be pleased by any sign of traditional behaviour.

It has been pointed out that the Bene Israel marriage ceremony is performed 'according to the Law of Moses and Israel'; and that among the Bene Israel as among other practising Jews the legitimizing rite of marriage is the religious ceremony.

But it should not be inferred from this that the form the family takes must also be the same. The family most common in the West and therefore most common among Western Jews, namely the relatively small, two-generation unit of parents and children, is not the only type of family in the world—nor the only type of family proper within Jewry.

NOTES

1. Kehimkar, ibid. pp. 128–9.
2. Kehimkar, ibid. pp. 129, 130–1.
3. Kehimkar, ibid. p. 58.
4. This is somewhat in contrast to Hindu practice. Thus in his *Caste and Kinship in Central India*, pp. 25–6, A. C. Mayer writes, 'There is patrilineal affiliation when informal unions openly occur across caste lines. Although there is no recognized marriage between people of different

castes, lovers sometimes live together and produce children who then belong to their progenitor's caste . . . as a kind of "second class member" . . . The cases where a person belongs only to his mother's caste are rare. They occur when a child is born to a widow or divorced woman by an unknown progenitor, or one who does not openly reside with her. . . . Such people are frequently allowed by their mother's kinsmen and fellow-villagers to act as though they were members of the mother's caste. . . . But this aid is purely gratuitous. The mother's kin need not acknowledge the child as a fellow-caste mate. . . .' In Judaism, however, the child of a Jewish mother by a non-Jew is not dependent upon the compassion of the mother's kin—regardless of the reaction of the mother's kin, the child is a full member of the group.

5. Similarly, Maurice Freedman in *A Minority in Britain*, London, 1955, p. 234, writes, '. . . Jews seem to marry out more than Jewesses, and this fact, presumably, reflects the differential social freedom of the sexes among Jews.' Again, A. C. Mayer in *A Report on the East Indian Community in Vancouver*, Working Paper, Institute of Social and Economic Research, University of British Columbia, 1959, pp. 18–19, relates that intermarriage seems to occur more often between East Indian men and white women. 'This is probably partly because East Indian women have less chance to meet outsiders, and also because they are said to enter such marriages more cautiously than men. For they know that if the match breaks up, they are more likely to hold custody of the children, with the problems that this entails.' (I wonder whether girls marry out less also because they are more subject to parental pressures and more fearful of being disowned by their families and shunned by the community than men.)

6. While working among the Bene Israel in Israel I encountered a member of the group who had married a Chinese woman in Calcutta and brought her with him to Israel. At that time many Bene Israel were exceedingly unhappy and determined to return to India. The Chinese woman, however, condemned them for arousing antipathy and for magnifying incidents of discrimination that did occur.

7. For the ban on polygyny among Western Jews, see above p. 30. For Ashkenazim, see above p. 51, n. 26.

8. Kehimkar, ibid. p. 108. Characteristically Kehimkar tries to show that Bene Israel customs are in accord with those of ancient Israel, in this case that the behaviour of Bene Israel polygynists is in accordance with the Mishna, the oldest collection, apart from the Pentateuch, of Jewish legislative writing.

9. In India, Jews (like Muslims) are governed by their religious laws, and polygyny is not banned for them.

10. Kehimkar, ibid. pp. 108–9.

11. See above, pp. 24, 25–26.

12. Kehimkar, ibid. pp. 56–7.

13. Kehimkar, ibid. p. 231. (For the military past of the Bene Israel, see above, p. 39 and p. 49, n. 10.)

14. There may well be more than three Bene Israel households in Bombay in which all married sons have remained with their parents, but their number is likely to be exceedingly small. Many Bene Israel told me that, as they knew I was interested in the 'old ways', they would inform me whenever they came across a traditional joint household. In fact, it was in this way that I first came across the three traditional joint households.

(But I dare say that I would have encountered them in any case because the members thereof were regular attendants at the synagogue with which I was most closely associated.) On the other hand, on a number of occasions some informants tried to pass off contemporary joint households as traditional ones. When reproached for the deception, they said, 'We only did it to please you.'

15. I had considerable contact with another 107 households in the Konkan, Poona, Karachi, and Delhi. And while the traditional joint household is less rare in the Konkan, even there some of the married sons prefer to set up a home of their own or move to Bombay—especially if they have married Bombay girls and have reason to believe that the wives' parents will help them to find accommodation and work.

16. Kehimkar, ibid. p. 109.

8
The Synagogue

Originally the word 'synagogue'—a Greek word—referred simply to a religious meeting; later it came to mean a building. Certainly the synagogue is the foremost religious institution in Jewish life, a place of public prayer and frequently also a centre for other religious and communal activities.

It probably had its beginnings during the Babylonian Captivity when the exiles met on Sabbaths and festivals in an effort to keep alive their hopes and their religious differences from the peoples about them. This form of worship was brought to Judaea after the return from the Babylonian Captivity; Ezra and the Scribes introduced into these meetings the custom of reading from the sacred books, thus starting Judaism on the unique development of study as worship. By the time the second Temple was destroyed, the synagogue had a fixed ritual, contributed most to the religious and literary education of young and old, and proved itself capable of keeping Judaism alive despite the loss of political autonomy. Both Christianity and Islam have used synagogal forms in the development of the worship of church and mosque.

According to Bene Israel history their first synagogue was established in Bombay in 1796. And although Kehimkar asserts that 'it was no doubt the first occasion when they united in congregational worship ever since they left their mother-country',[1] it is exceedingly difficult to believe that for many centuries Bene Israel did not come together in prayer and worship—even if they did so at the home of some prominent member of the community rather than in a building especially erected for this purpose and designated 'synagogue'. But then, the dispersed condition of the Bene Israel during their Konkan days probably did not encourage the building of a synagogue.

Nowadays there are four Bene Israel synagogues and three Bene Israel prayer-halls in Bombay—a prayer-hall differs from a synagogue in that it consists of but one or two rooms rented for purposes of worship rather than a whole building; management and membership fees of the prayer-halls are the same as at the synagogues; and, moreover, some synagogues started as prayer-halls. One of these prayer-halls serves the Jewish Religious Union which seeks its inspiration in Liberal Judaism and is associated with the World Union of Progressive Judaism. There are also a number of Bene Israel synagogues and prayer-halls in various parts of the country where Bene Israel happen to be living, such as in the Konkan, Poona, Thana, Delhi, etc.

All Bene Israel places of worship in Bombay, including the one serving the Jewish Religious Union, are situated in the poor areas of the town where most members of the community live.[2] Of the two Baghdadi places of worship in Bombay, one is in a poor area—the Jewish neighbourhood—where most members of the Baghdadi community live, the other is in Fort, close to the boundary with Colaba, a much more prosperous and certainly more fashionable district.

SYNAGOGUE MEMBERSHIP

As all Bene Israel synagogues and prayer-halls are in the poor areas of the town, and, moreover, most Bene Israel travel on Sabbaths and festivals,[3] proximity is not of the utmost importance when deciding on which place of worship to join. Bene Israel may join one place of worship rather than another because their parents were or are associated with it, or because it has better facilities, allowing more people to be invited to the celebrations following upon weddings, circumcision, redemption of the first-born son, and so on. Again, they are not averse to changing from one synagogue to another because of quarrels or unwillingness to accept a position in the background or because their friends have changed to another synagogue, and so on.[4] But (excepting the Jewish Religious Union whose members belong to the most educated and professionally most successful section of the community and which members of the clerk section might hesitate to join) there are no preferred or fashionable places of worship. The important point is to be a member of a synagogue rather than a member of a particular synagogue. In any case, members are not assigned seats, so that being a member in one place of worship does not debar one from occupying a seat in another. Again, even members of the Jewish Religious Union may attend Orthodox places of worship. Indeed, some members of the Jewish Religious Union are members of the Orthodox places of worship.

Even considering the harassed financial circumstances of many Bene Israel, membership of the synagogue is cheap—Rs. 3 per annum—so that only the completely destitute are prevented from joining. In most cases, membership is held by the senior male of the household. Sons may join in their own right either before or soon after marriage, else after setting up a home of their own. Except for those 'who haven't got round to it yet' and some who fail to find any satisfaction in the life of the community, adult males do at some time in their lives become members of a place of worship. Occasionally women—usually single or widowed— join in their own right.

THE ACTIVITIES OF THE SYNAGOGUE

The following account of the activities of the Bene Israel synagogue is concerned with the Orthodox places of worship only; the Jewish Religious Union will be discussed in a later section. However, it ought to be pointed out that in the last few years there has been a split in the Orthodox section. In an attempt to unite their places of worship and increase contact with Jewish communities elsewhere, aid was enlisted from America. As a result, instead of one federation, two have been established: one, the United Synagogue of India, has secured affiliation to the World Council of Synagogues, whose main support is the Conservative Jewish movement in America; the other, the Union of Orthodox Jewish Congregations in India, is linked to the Union of Orthodox Jewish Congregations of America. But as B. J. Israel writes, 'The irony is that, whatever ideological differences may underlie the separate existence of the two supporting American organizations, there is absolutely no difference in belief and practice between Bene Israel synagogues and prayer-halls affiliated to one body and those affiliated to the other.'[5] My own impression is that this correctly characterizes the situation. It is in fact possible that once the initial enthusiasm has evaporated, and aid is no longer given, the affiliation may cease. Hence in the following account no distinction is made between the United Synagogue of India and the Union of Orthodox Jewish Congregations of India. Again, this account concentrates on social relations rather than on ritual acts.

The obvious activity of the synagogue is that of conducting religious services. Services are held in the morning and evening of each weekday and on Sabbaths and festivals. Except on festivals and on special occasions—such as *Selichoth,* penitential prayers recited daily at 4 a.m. from before the New Year till the Day of Atonement, at which if one is but a few minutes late there is hardly any standing room to be obtained even in the women's gallery—many services are poorly attended. They are conducted by the *Chazan,* Reader, a paid official. As among the Baghdadi community of Bombay, there is no rabbi. (Only the Liberal Jewish movement has secured the services of a rabbi.)

The poor attendance at many services does not mean that the majority of Bene Israel only rarely set foot in the synagogue compound. For the Bene Israel synagogue is the place where communal business is discussed, where notices of interest to members of the community may be displayed, where the children receive their religious instruction, in whose yard some sit about all day and the poor of the community sleep at night, and so on. Moreover, the synagogue is the place where many Bene Israel celebrate important occasions in the individual life cycle. Indeed, while there are times when even the most popular and fashionable places of worship in London give the impression of being defunct, there is always something going on in the Bene Israel synagogue.

A number of informants, when suddenly asked 'Why did you join the synagogue?' replied 'It's cheaper to be a member.' It is a strange answer—but makes sense nevertheless. Many rituals in the life of an individual require the services of the Reader of the synagogue or his Assistant and the attendance of kinsfolk and friends. Now those keenest on observing many rituals are often among the poorest members of the community, those whose homes usually consist of only one small room. Hence most rituals are performed and celebrated on synagogue premises, the fee for which is reduced for members. Obviously those intent on observing the various rituals are unlikely to be deterred by the cost of the synagogue hall—a large room with cooking facilities within the synagogue compound—probably the least expensive item of the whole venture; Nevertheless, it may help to encourage individuals to join the synagogue sooner rather than later.

CIRCUMCISION

Circumcision, the rite which symbolizes the entrance of the Jewish male child into the Abrahamic covenant, takes place on the eighth day after birth (subject to the satisfactory state of the child's health). There were times in Jewish history when the rite of circumcision was performed at the risk of martyrdom, and no doubt this circumstance has conferred a special sanctity upon it —its observance is sometimes the sole remaining token of allegiance to Judaism, after all other observances have been discarded.

In the West circumcision tends to take place in the hospital. But Bene Israel say that the hospital authorities do not allow circumcision to be performed on their premises nor do they allow the child to be taken away for the rite and returned after it; as a result, the mother of a son must leave the hospital seven days after the birth of the child. Circumcision among the Bene Israel almost always takes place in the synagogue.

The evening before the day of circumcision a few men, kinsfolk and friends, will go to the synagogue to place a copy of the Scriptures on the chair of Elijah the Prophet (according to a Jewish legend Elijah the Prophet, in his mystic capacity of 'Angel of the Covenant', is an invisible participant at every circumcision ceremony) and deposit a citron which will be cut and distributed after the ceremony. Some Bene Israel complained that 'The bazaar people know quite well that we must have a citron for circumcision and so will try to push up the price.' Having already come to the synagogue in order to prepare for the circumcision next day, the men may remain for the evening service after which the father of the child will provide them with refreshments in the synagogue hall.

The circumcision ceremony will be well attended; kinsfolk and friends will come along; sometimes the synagogue Beadle will be hired to go around the various buildings in which Bene Israel live to announce the birth of the child, the time of circumcision, and to invite the members of the community to witness the child's initiation into the covenant of Abraham. After the circumcision sweets and pieces of citron will be distributed among all present. But the main feast will be in the evening, usually in the synagogue hall, to which the circumcisor, kinsfolk and friends, and especially young couples who are hoping for a son, will be invited. Not infrequently the father of the child will present the communal orphanage with a chicken in honour of the occasion. As elsewhere, the occasion of circumcision is considered a suitable opportunity for conferring a name upon the infant (but this is not an integral part of the ceremony of circumcision).

THE MARRIAGE CEREMONY

Only the most important festivals and the *Selichoth* services bring more people to the synagogue than does a marriage ceremony. Nor is this surprising: marriage involves two sets of circles, the kinsfolk and friends of the bride and the groom. Moreover, while non-Jews are not encouraged to be present in the synagogue during prayers proper, non-Jewish friends may be invited to attend the marriage ceremony in the synagogue. But then, while other rituals are peculiar to the Jewish community, all communities have ceremonies solemnizing the marriage so that the nature of the ceremony will be explicit to all.

Like circumcision, the religious marriage ceremony is observed by all elements of the community. Like circumcision, the marriage ceremony involves the use of the synagogue proper and the services of its officials. But while the wealthy will hold the receptions following upon the marriage ceremony in a fashionable club in town, the great majority of the Bene Israel will hire the synagogue hall or, if it is not available or considered too small to hold all those invited, some other hall in the neighbourhood.

During my stay in Bombay two Bene Israel marriages were solemnized in the Baghdadi synagogue situated in the Jewish neighbourhood. It was said that no Bene Israel synagogue would have been large enough to hold all those invited to witness the ceremony—and certainly the Baghdadi synagogue was filled to capacity. Again in both cases it was said that the Bene Israel couples would not have been allowed to hire the Baghdadi synagogue if they had not belonged to families prominent in Bombay life—and certainly both couples were exceedingly well connected. In both cases the marriage ceremony was conducted by Bene

Israel officials. Informants said that, however well connected, Bene Israel would not have been allowed to hire the Baghdadi synagogue prior to Indian Independence and that even now Bene Israel would not be allowed to hire the Baghdadi synagogue in Fort. (But a recent communication states that Bene Israel are now able to hire even the Baghdadi synagogue in Fort.) However, there is no trend for well connected Bene Israel to marry in the Baghdadi synagogue: equally well connected couples marry in the Bene Israel synagogue.

DEATH

All Bene Israel places of worship participate in the administration of the communal cemetery. But it is usually the Reader of the synagogue of which the deceased was a member who will officiate at the funeral. Members of the synagogue, kinsfolk, and both Jewish and non-Jewish friends will attend the funeral.

For seven days after burial kinsfolk and friends will go to the mourners' home for the morning and evening prayers; a quorum of ten male Jews (over the age of thirteen) is necessary for the recital of these prayers. But during the eleven months after the death the male mourners will attend the synagogue services to recite the *kaddish* prayer—which is not a prayer for the dead, but rather a dedication to the service of the Lord and a declaration that the mourners do not murmur against the Lord's decree. Thus, as elsewhere among Jews, memorial prayers help to swell synagogue attendances.

Kehimkar relates that when the Baghdadis first came to Bombay they buried their dead in the Bene Israel cemetery; but later 'wrote to Government for permission to erect a partition wall to divide the Indian Jews' cemetery from that of the foreign Jews. But Government by their letter of 17 February 1837 declined to comply with the request.'[6] Nowadays the Baghdadis maintain a cemetery of their own.

OTHER RITUALS IN THE LIFE OF THE INDIVIDUAL

Engagements, festivities before the marriage and on the days following upon it, redemption of the first-born son, the ceremony of the first head-shaving of the child, and so on, do not involve

I

the synagogue proper though they may take place in the synagogue hall.

Among Jews elsewhere the redemption of the first-born son is performed on the thirty-first day of his birth, in accordance with Numbers 18:16, 'from a month old shalt thou redeem them'; however, should the thirty-first day fall on a Sabbath or festival, the ceremony is postponed until the following day. Kehimkar, who is usually quick to point out that Bene Israel religious observances are consonant with those of their co-religionists, relates that the redemption of the first-born son ceremony takes place after forty days 'when his mother is purified'.[7] In other words, according to Kehimkar the observance of Leviticus 12:2, 4—'If a woman be delivered, and bear a man-child, then she shall be unclean seven days. . . . And she shall continue in the blood of purification three and thirty days; she shall touch no hallowed thing, nor come into the sanctuary, until the days of her purification be fulfilled'—results in the postponement of the redemption of the first-born son ceremony. But whatever may have been the custom in Kehimkar's days, Bene Israel nowadays perform this ceremony at any convenient time before marriage.

Apart from the redemption of the first-born son, many Bene Israel no longer perform all the rituals in the life of the individual —the poor may find them much too costly and the comparatively wealthy Bene Israel who could afford them have neither the time nor the inclination for them. Besides, it is argued that many of these ceremonies are not Jewish in origin but 'merely local usages' and should be abandoned.

While among many other Jewish communities the *Bar Mitzvah* ('Son of the Commandment' originally applied to every adult Jew, but since the fourteenth century specially made to refer to a Jewish boy attaining the age of thirteen) is an occasion which brings large numbers of kinsfolk and friends to the synagogue to witness the 'calling-up' of the boy to the Reading of the Law on the Sabbath following his thirteenth birthday, among the Bene Israel this ceremony is virtually ignored. During my stay in India only one *Bar Mitzvah* was celebrated. I was not in Bombay at the time, but was told that there was a large attendance at the synagogue that Sabbath 'because it is so rare that many people had never before witnessed a *Bar Mitzvah* ceremony'. The father of the *Bar Mitzvah* boy earns part of his income from the sale of Hebrew books, and it was suggested that 'having so many Hebrew books at his home stimulated him to observe a more orthodox way of life'.[8]

S. D. Goitein relates that there was no *Bar Mitzvah* ceremony among the Yemenite Jews; and he suggests that this step from childhood to maturity was not stressed because there was no transition: from his earliest youth the child took part in adult life.[9] My own impression is that the Bene Israel do not observe the *Bar Mitzvah* ceremony because this community's main guide to religious practices is the Pentateuch—in which the *Bar Mitzvah* is not explicitly mentioned.

RELIGIOUS EDUCATION

It is a common feature of Jewish communities that the synagogue makes some arrangements for the religious education of the children of its members—and the Bene Israel are no exception.

In some Bene Israel synagogues religious instruction forms part of the duties of the Reader, in others someone may be especially employed for this task. In one synagogue an enthusiastic member of the congregation—a bachelor—gives his services free of charge.

Classes are open to both boys and girls, but tend to be poorly attended. In any case, instruction is designed to teach the children only to read the prayers and to chant the traditional tunes; but few ever learn the meaning of what they read. However, most children read so fluently and accurately that it is difficult to believe that they are not aware of the meaning of what they read.

But poor attendance at synagogue classes does not mean that only few children learn to read Hebrew. For many Bene Israel, in spite of their depressed financial position, have their children privately taught. Moreover, those attending the Bene Israel school or the Baghdadi school receive a modicum of Hebrew and religious instruction. Again, many Bene Israel children attend the Hebrew classes organized by the Jewish Agency-subsidized teacher in Bombay.

SYNAGOGUE LEADERSHIP

Control of the synagogues used to be in the hands of the most educated members of the community—those who held good positions in Government service and were, moreover, wealthy enough to make handsome contributions to the funds and activities of the synagogues. It is said that there was much rivalry for office, each office seeker competing for the support of the rank and file, and that as a result of these unseemly struggles the most educated element of the Bene Israel lost the trust of the rank and file and the leadership of the community. However that may have been, the most educated members of the community no longer struggle for control of the synagogues. Indeed, it is said that the university-educated Bene Israel in the professions and in the higher ranks of the public services, commercial corporations and industry would stand very little chance of getting elected. For there is a certain antagonism between the university-educated Bene Israel and the clerks as well as a recognition that the former are much too preoccupied with secular affairs to give sufficient time and energy to the business of the synagogues. Nowadays, then, it is the clerk element which is in charge of the synagogues—and therefore of much of communal life.

Synagogue affairs are managed by a committee elected by paid up members present at the annual general meeting. Synagogue membership is cheap—only Rs 3 a year—so that it would be possible for those who want to get elected to persuade their friends and those of their kinsfolk with whom they are on good terms to join just before the election and vote for them. To avoid such obvious gerrymandering some synagogues rule that only those who have been members for at least six months may vote in the elections; even so it would still be possible for a candidate to persuade his friends to join some months in advance—but informants held that only a very determined candidate would indulge in such forethought and only very few people would be willing to get involved with him. During my stay in Bombay only one synagogue election threatened to engender much heat; but in the end the candidate to whom a number of members objected decided not to stand for office and the election passed almost unnoticed.

Some committee members are appreciated for giving of their time and energy to the affairs of the synagogue, a few are held to be 'busybodies' who tend to make a nuisance of themselves; but apart from those who are employed by the synagogue—such as the Reader, his Assistant, the Clerk, the Beadle—and receive their orders from committee members, the latter are treated with little deference by those who elected them. For it is only too well recognized that it is but one's equals, the rank and file of the community, and not those engaged in prestigeful professions, who occupy themselves with synagogue affairs. Indeed, those who would hesitate to allow their children to marry Kala Bene Israel would nevertheless vote for Kala in synagogue elections. In fact, during my stay in Bombay the President of one of the Bene Israel synagogues was a member of the Kala element.

However, the fact that members of the synagogue committee are not treated with great deference does not mean that their activities are unimportant. On the contrary, apart from seeing to it that services are held regularly, that the synagogue and its officials are at the disposal of those who require them for rituals such as circumcision and marriage, that the children receive religious instruction, the committee administers the funds of the synagogue and decides on the contributions to be made to the educational and charitable undertakings of the community.

Although membership is cheap, the synagogues, unlike other communal undertakings, are comparatively wealthy. For they derive their income not only from membership fees but also from fees paid for the hire of synagogue premises for the performance of rituals in the life of the individual, from donations made by those who wish to recite some of the prayers during services on Sabbaths and festivals, and so on. Moreover, gifts made to the synagogues over the years seem to have been well invested and help to swell their incomes. From this income the synagogues are expected to make annual contributions to the communal school, to the communal home for orphans, to the maintenance of the cemetery, to give to the destitutes before Passover and the New Year, etc. But in return for these contributions, and according to their size, the synagogues send representatives to the committees of these undertakings. Obviously the size of the contribution depends on the wealth of each synagogue—but I have heard it said that if the committee of a particular synagogue aspires to have an important voice in the management of a particular undertaking, it will concentrate its resources on that undertaking rather than on another.

Not surprisingly, then, members of the committees are not obliged to be orthodox in their private lives. They are not elected for their adherence to religious practices nor for their power to provide spiritual leadership but for their ability to organize and manage the affairs of the synagogue and to administer its finances. And as financial contributions to communal undertakings confer the right to send representatives to the committees of these undertakings, it may well be said that the synagogue committees not only administer the affairs of the congregations that elect them, but also participate in the management of all important communal undertakings.

It is time now to turn to the Jewish Religious Union, the small group of Bene Israel who profess Liberal Judaism, that is, a Judaism consciously adapted to the needs of a modernized life.

THE JEWISH RELIGIOUS UNION

Members of the Jewish Religious Union seek their inspiration in the teachings of Claude Montefiore, the founder of the Liberal Jewish movement in England.

Liberal Judaism began with the emancipation of the Jews from the ghetto. Jews identifying themselves with the cultural environment of their country felt in some of the practices of the Synagogue an incompatibility with their new life. As a result, they altered or abolished them. Later Liberal Judaism developed a new attitude to the Talmud, denying the authority ascribed to it by Orthodox Judaism. Indeed, according to Liberal Jewish teachings, Bible, Talmud, and Jewish tradition constitute a guide, not an absolute authority, for present Jewish thought and practice.

No doubt the founders of the Jewish Religious Union in Bombay were animated by spiritual interest; certainly the beliefs of Liberal Bene Israel do not differ from those held by Liberal Jews elsewhere. Nevertheless, Orthodox Bene Israel hold that it is social status rather than religious doctrine which differentiates them from the small group which professes Liberal Judaism. Thus the bulk of the Bene Israel look upon membership of the Jewish Religious Union as a symbol of social status rather than as an indication of an interest in Judaism. Nor is this surprising.

Membership of the Jewish Religious Union—established over forty years ago—is drawn mainly from the Bene Israel in prestigeful professions. It is not suggested that all educationally and professionally distinguished Bene Israel are members of the Jewish Religious Union but rather that those who do not enjoy educational and professional superiority only rarely apply for membership. As a result, membership of the Union is restricted to a small section of the community.

Its religious services are conducted mainly in English; and although the Union aimed at ultimately switching over to Marathi, this has not yet been done after a lapse of some four decades. From time to time the Union arranged for rabbis from England and America to conduct its services during the High Holy Days, and for a while it secured the services of a rabbi throughout the year.

During my stay in Bombay, services were held in a small room in the communal neighbourhood. Since then the Union has acquired a more spacious prayer-hall, also in the communal neighbourhood, and has been joined by some of the better-educated clerk element. But I have heard it said that the latter joined by invitation rather than on their own initiative, and, moreover, that they were invited to join not so much in order to make the movement more representative but rather to help increase the income of the Union.

Members of the Orthodox Bene Israel places of worship told me, 'Some Liberal Bene Israel are just as orthodox as Orthodox Bene Israel—and a few Liberals are even more orthodox than Orthodox Bene Israel.' Moreover, membership of the Jewish Religious Union does not act as a barrier to an appreciation of traditional services and occasional attendances at Orthodox places of worship. Indeed, some members of the Jewish Religious Union have retained their membership of Orthodox places of worship; a few members of the Jewish Religious Union have remained members of the committees of Orthodox places of worship; occasionally a member of the Jewish Religious Union may preside over a function in an Orthodox place of worship, and so on. Certainly the rabbis who have hitherto served the Jewish Religious Union have exerted an influence on Bene Israel communal life beyond their own congregation. It is indeed recognized that the division between Orthodox and Liberal Bene Israel reflects not so much differences in religious principles and practices but differences in education, occupation, recreation, intellectual interests, influence, income, prestige, etc. Thus membership of the Jewish Religious Union suggests a solidity of social status rather than a new theological adjustment or an abandonment of burdensome religious observances. (Indeed, in spite of my strong leanings towards Orthodox Judaism I was immensely flattered when told that I was fit to be a member of the Liberal group. Admittedly, this view was expressed mainly by Orthodox Bene Israel; it was only after I had been in Bombay for many months that some members of the Jewish Religious Union—after an investigation of my secular education and intellectual interests and in spite of my leanings towards Orthodoxy which must have served as an irritant to those adhering to modernized Judaism— pronounced that they regarded me as qualified to join their group.)

Members of the Jewish Religious Union, being in prestigeful occupations and therefore earning an income which gives them a security far beyond the mere ability to care for fundamental physical needs, belong to the affluent section of the community. But they do not control wealth nor have they been wealthy in the past. They do not enjoy economic power. They are unable to give heavy support to communal undertakings. They cannot employ or sack. The small number of Bene Israel in business undertakings of their own, and those who hold high positions in large concerns, hesitate to employ co-members—fearing that the egalitarian values of the Bene Israel would make it difficult to enter into and accept philosophically a relationship of inequality between co-members. I only heard of two Bene Israel who went out of their way to secure employment for co-members. It was said that they did so in return for votes at communal elections. Obviously I do not know whether there is any truth whatever in these allegations, but I do know that since their retirement they have found it somewhat difficult to get elected.

True, those who are lawyers and doctors can render services which people need. But Bene Israel are not the only lawyers in Bombay; in any case, many Bene Israel prefer to consult lawyers who are not members of the community. And while Bene Israel doctors give of their time and skill to the poor of the community, it is said that they prefer to be appealed to on human grounds rather than on grounds of communal solidarity.

Again, members of the Jewish Religious Union do not dominate the communal scene. They do not organize communal activities.

Bene Israel know that secular preoccupations engage the time and energy of the most educated element of the community; indeed I have heard it said, 'All they would have time for is to patronize us, and our Bene Israel are much too democratic to put up with that!' Members of the Jewish Religious Union may occasionally be asked to grace a communal meeting by presiding over it (even in the compound of an Orthodox synagogue), but they do not represent the community *vis-à-vis* Jewish visitors from abroad—meetings in honour of the latter are presided over by those who organize them, the clerk element. No wonder, then, that Western Jewish visitors get the impression that Bene Israel are as 'poor as church mice', 'the world's poorest Jews', and so on—even though some of these visitors do meet a number of those engaged in prestigeful professions and in enjoyment of an income far above that of the clerk element. For the highly educated and comparatively wealthy Bene Israel do not represent the community—it is the clerks who are in charge of organized life within communal boundaries.

Members of the Jewish Religious Union do not act as 'ambassadors to the Gentiles': the majority of Bene Israel do not look upon the better educated and better off as guardians of the community's relations with the wider world (but then, neither do they live in fear of being pounced upon by the wider world); they do not hold that the success of some Bene Israel in the wider world will benefit the community collectively. In any case, the successful Bene Israel are probably much too few in number to become representative of the community. No wonder then that on a number of occasions Hindu and Muslim acquaintances who have asked me how I had come to know this famous doctor or that well-known lawyer were rather surprised when told that I had encountered them in the course of a study of the Bene Israel community of which these individuals were members.

As among Western Jewries, those who have made a name for themselves in the wider world are treated with deference. But (and in this they differ from Western Jewries) they do not wield power in the community nor do they function as symbols of the community. For it is realized that the successful Bene Israel are involved in a wider world and no longer belong entirely to the community. It is not surprising then that in spite of their explicit departure from Orthodoxy, members of the Jewish Religious

Union are not charged with disloyalty to Judaism but with lack of adequate involvement in communal affairs.

RELIGIOUS BELIEFS AND PRACTICES

The description of the religious organization of the Bene Israel has led to a discussion of leadership and the basis of social status rather than an account of Bene Israel religious beliefs and practices. What, then, about the beliefs and practices which lie behind the religious organization?

Most members of the Orthodox places of worship shied away from the subject of Bene Israel belief. It is not a topic for discussion—and certainly not with me since it was held, that however enamoured of the community I appeared to be, I was after all a member of that section of Jewry which seemed forever to be examining Bene Israel on their knowledge of Judaism and awarding them bad marks for it. Nevertheless, some of those I knew best told me on their own initiative that all Bene Israel were immensely proud of being monotheists, and, moreover, that Orthodox Bene Israel believed what Orthodox Jews elsewhere believed—just as Liberal Bene Israel believed what Liberal Jews elsewhere believed. No doubt many Bene Israel knew less about Judaism than Jews elsewhere—but then Orthodox Bene Israel have no rabbis in their midst. But this lack of knowledge could not destroy the religious unity which is based on what differentiates Jews from other religious groups and on the fundamental agreement in the beliefs about God and the relations between Him and man.

In spite of their fervour for Jewish monotheism, Bene Israel do not dismiss other religions—whether monotheistic or not—as idle superstitions. For just as there is no suspiciousness and fear of the non-Jew—a consequence of Bene Israel lack of experience of hostility from the non-Jewish world—so there is no contempt for his values and beliefs. Indeed, many informants insisted that although Hindus were fond of idols their ideas were not really incompatible with a belief in a Supreme Being; moreover, many Hindus led a good life and were gentle and kind—perhaps more so than some of those who professed monotheism. Indeed, I was told that Hindus were much less given to violence than Muslims or even Bene Israel. Some informants emphasized that it was not that monotheism made for rowdyism, but that abstaining from eating meat probably accounted for the gentle nature of the Hindus. (A member of the community who is a policeman told me that he too found that Bene Israel and Muslims were much more given to violence than Hindus—and he said that a study of police records would confirm this view.) Again, unlike some sections of Jewry which lived in ghettos more or less unaware of the culture of the non-Jewish world, Bene Israel do not hold that, in comparison with the satisfying ritual of Judaism, the life of the non-Jew is empty of pleasurable ritual.

Orthodox places of worship tend to follow the liturgy of the Jews of Cochin—indeed, many of their synagogue Readers were Cochin Jews who helped to determine the final form that Bene Israel synagogue worship assumed. The services of the Jewish Religious Union follow the simpler forms of worship adopted by Liberal Jewish congregations in London. Again, while many of those professing Orthodox Judaism buy kosher meat, few Liberal Bene Israel observe the Jewish dietary regulations. On the other hand, virtually all Bene Israel travel on the Sabbath and accept employment which requires them to work on the Sabbath. (I only encountered one member of the community, a man then in his late seventies, who told me that he had never worked on the Sabbath and had in fact been out of work for nineteen years because of his unwillingness to accept employment that would force him to work on the Sabbath. His son, one of the few who attended the synagogue daily, morning and evening, confirmed this information, adding, 'He has always been difficult to get on with.')

The subordination of the requirements of Jewish law to secular compulsions is not peculiar to the Bene Israel: it also marks large sections of other Jewries. Again, elsewhere too membership of Orthodox places of worship does not necessarily imply strict adherence to Orthodox Jewish law. Nevertheless, many Orthodox Jews find it difficult to accept Bene Israel in the same way as they accept other Jews not strictly orthodox in their private lives. And even many non-Orthodox Jews find it difficult to accept Bene Israel as full co-religionists. The *religious* basis of the marginal status of this community within Jewry seems to rest on the suspicion that Bene Israel who have been isolated for centuries from the mainstream of Jewish life and influenced by a social system not usually associated with Judaism are likely to entertain beliefs

and practices which are 'positively' incompatible with Judaism—
a suspicion not borne out by the evidence.

Unlike Western Jewries, Bene Israel have no rabbis in their
midst. Unlike Western Jewries, Bene Israel have no élite based
on Jewish learning. Unlike Western Orthodox congregations,
Bene Israel Orthodox congregations can be thought of as identi-
cal: they cannot be distinguished by the level of ritual observance
of their members. Among the Bene Israel it is the rank and file
who are in charge of activities rather than, as among many Western
Jewries, the distinguished members of the congregations. As
used to be the case among Jewries elsewhere, there is among
the Bene Israel a general relation between social status and adherence to Liberal Judaism; elsewhere, however, the situation has
changed in that it is now not at all unusual to combine social
emergence with Orthodoxy. Finally, as used to be the case among
Jewries elsewhere, among the Bene Israel the synagogue remains
in a very real sense the crucial centre of the community.

NOTES

1. Kehimkar, ibid. p. 65.
2. I stress the fact that even the group involved in Liberal Judaism wor-
   ships in the poor district of the town because it is unusual. As Freedman,
   op. cit. p. 233, writes, the synagogues associated with the Liberal and
   Reform movements 'are to be found in areas of London which suggest
   a relative prosperity and solidity of social status'. He adds, in a footnote, 'The Liberal synagogue in East London (E.1), which seems a
   contradiction to the general relation between middle-class status and
   adherence to modernized Judaism, is the St George's Settlement
   Synagogue, founded in 1925 under the auspices of the West London
   and Liberal Jewish Synagogues.' In India, too, there is a strong relation
   between upper-middle-class status and adherence to modernized
   Judaism; nevertheless the place of worship of the group involved in it
   is in a poor area of the town.
3. But then the great majority of Jews in Bombay travel on the Sabbath.
   Indeed, Bombay Jewry has produced a unique curiosity of Jewish
   observance—a tramway ticket sold to Jews on Friday and allowing
   them to travel on the Sabbath without paying for it on this day on
   which money should not be handled. (Obviously, I am not competent
   to comment on the validity of this departure from the traditional pro-
   hibition of travelling on the Sabbath.) It is said that some Orthodox

Jews took advantage of this concession; but the bulk of Bombay Jewry did not avail itself of it and these tickets are no longer issued.

4. The President of one of the Bene Israel places of worship told me, 'Today if someone comes and says he wants to change his synagogue membership we at once suspect that he owes his first synagogue money: people promise donations in return for the privilege of reciting some of the prayers and then some don't pay; when they owe a lot and cannot pay it, they may try to change their synagogue. We don't encourage this sort of thing!'

5. B. J. Israel, ibid. p. 19.

6. Kehimkar, ibid. p. 163.

7. Kehimkar, ibid. p. 124.

8. Some, somewhat unkindly, suggested that the father of the *Bar Mitzvah* boy hoped that attendance at the ceremony would stimulate the sale of Hebrew books.

9. S. D. Goitein, 'Jewish Education in the Yemen as an Archetype of Traditional Jewish Education' in *Between Past and Future* (ed. Frankenstein), Jerusalem, 1953, pp. 115–16.

9
Educational and Charitable Associations

The first needs of a Jewish community are a place of worship and a place of burial. Upon first coming to Bombay Bene Israel probably assembled for worship at the home of a prominent family of the community; their first permanent place of worship, The Gate of Mercy Synagogue, was established in 1796. As for a place of burial, Kehimkar writes, 'We at one time entertained the hope of fixing the date of our ancestors' coming to the City of Bombay from the Konkan for the first time, by ascertaining the date of a free grant of a site by the Government to our people shortly after their arrival in that place.'[1] And though Kehimkar was unable to establish the exact date of the grant of a site for purposes of burial, it seems certain that the Bene Israel, who began settling in Bombay about the middle of the eighteenth century, obtained their first burial ground there at least two decades before they obtained their first permanent place of worship.

But as a Jewish community grows in numbers and becomes more firmly established, subsidiary undertakings soon follow, such as the provision for the education of its children and associations to insure its poor and its incapable against destitution. This chapter, then, will concern itself with a description and discussion of Bene Israel associations, most of which came into being between the latter half of the nineteenth and the early part of the twentieth century, a period during which the number of Bene Israel in Bombay ranged from 2,300 to 5,000.

Although this chapter is concerned with the existing associations only, reference will be made to the Bene Israel Conference and the All India Israelite League which, while no longer on the communal map, represented serious attempts to produce a central authority to direct communal policy. Moreover, some of the existing associations came into being as a result of these two rival bodies.

Clearly, then, the period between the latter half of the nineteenth and the early part of the twentieth century was one in which efforts were made to come together and discuss communal problems, co-operate to further projects, and raise comparatively large sums towards their realization. Indeed, some informants held that it would take 'a systematic effort just to remember some of the things attempted'. But as it was only in the middle of the eighteenth century that Bene Israel slowly began to leave their Konkan homes, the latter half of the nineteenth century was still an early period in the life of the Bombay community, and Bene Israel had to find out by experience what they could and could not do.

It was also a period of Bene Israel fervour for education, a period in which they did remarkably well in the pursuit of scholarship. For example, an informant told me that in the early 1920s in one English High School for Indian girls, where only a quarter of the pupils were Bene Israel, out of twenty-seven scholarships awarded for merit, the Bene Israel girls held nineteen. Another informant told me, 'It is not that our Bene Israel are now less brilliant than before and therefore hold fewer scholarships than before, but that the number of scholarships seems to have diminished—perhaps they are not as justly distributed as hitherto.' Again, this informant who holds a high position in a prestigeful profession said that while he had been educated at the expense of his father, the majority of Bene Israel in prestigeful professions had achieved their education by means of scholarships—'something on which our Bene Israel can now no longer rely'. In fact, the number of scholarships has vastly increased—but, then, so has the number of applicants.[2]

Finally, it was a period of friction and contention between the educated members of the community. For the creation of the various associations resulted in a struggle for their control, in opposing factions and break-aways. Dissension brought disillusion; and many of the associations which were started ceased functioning almost at once. An informant with a clear memory of the Bene Israel condition in the early twentieth century said, 'No amount of material gain can make up for the moral harm done by the embittered hostility into which the friction and contention among the leading men of the community developed. If it was not possible to work together, it should not have been impossible to work apart, according to each one's lights, without going out of one's way to obstruct good work done by either party.'

It is said that it was the unseemly manoeuvres and counter-manoeuvres of the educated members of the community on the platforms of the Bene Israel Conference and the All India Israelite League which deprived them of the trust of the rank and file. Unable to believe any longer in the purity of the motives of the educated section, the rank and file decided to take over communal control.

Leaving aside considerations of purity of motives, there has certainly been a change in the mood of the community. On the one hand, the rank and file, partly as a result of a rise in their educational attainments, expects a greater say in communal affairs. On the other hand, the most educated section of the Bene Israel has withdrawn from communal affairs: although wealthy members occasionally contribute to communal projects, as a group they do not compete with the clerks for communal control, preferring to confine themselves to such charities as the Education Fund and the Stree Mandal, charities which they founded. But these are charities which—at least at present—are of no great consequence in the community; their importance would appear to lie in providing some points of contact between the educated section of the community and the rank and file.

Thus it is the rank and file which controls not only the synagogues but also the home for orphans and destitutes, the great part of the offices of the school and the co-operative society. And whatever the reservations some have about the administration of the synagogues, the home for orphans and destitutes, the school, and the co-operative society, it is agreed that it is these associations which the Bene Israel cannot afford to lose—for they mark out the sphere of communal life, indeed they keep it in existence.

THE BENE ISRAEL SCHOOL

B. J. Israel writes, 'By the middle of the nineteenth century missionary influence began perceptibly to decline . . . the missionaries gradually withdrew from the field of primary education. . . . In secondary schools, also, the missionaries learned to confine themselves to strictly secular subjects, subjected as they were to a rigid grant-in-aid code prescribed by a Government conscious, particularly after the Indian Mutiny of 1857, of the political dangers of a Christian bias in education.'[3] I have heard it said that it was because Bene Israel could no longer rely on getting their Hebrew education from the missionaries that they were obliged to open a school of their own in which their children could receive instruction in the religion and language of their ancestors. One cannot help wondering whether Bene Israel are not exaggerating the missionaries' contribution to their religious revival: certainly in the second half of the nineteenth century the Baghdadis had begun to settle in large numbers in Bombay and Cochin Jews were acting as Readers in Bene Israel synagogues, contributing to the Bene Israel religious revival—perhaps Bene Israel prefer to feel obliged to the missionaries, with whom they have always been on good terms, rather than to their co-religionists with whom their relationship has not always been a happy one.[4]

Hence, to supply the want of a communal school where the children of the Bene Israel could receive both religious and secular instruction, some philanthropic men of the community, headed by H. S. Kehimkar, formed an association called 'The Bene Israel Benevolent Society for Promoting Education', and opened a small primary school in 1875. As this modest school was soon found to be inadequate to meet the needs of the community, Kehimkar appealed for assistance to the Anglo-Jewish Association of London, and with their aid, together with the help of a grant from the Government, subscriptions from the synagogues, in particular from The Gate of Mercy Synagogue, the oldest Bene Israel synagogue and the one with the greatest resources, and donations from individuals, the school in 1881 developed from a primary into an Anglo-Vernacular school, calling itself 'The Israelite School'. It was located in a rented house, in an area which informants described as 'the heart of the Bene Israel ghetto'. Small fees began to be charged in 1886. By 1892 the venture had developed into a full-blown High School teaching both boys and girls up to the Matriculation Standard of the University of Bombay. In 1896, as a result of the indefatigable efforts of Kehimkar, the school secured a building of its own at Mazgaon—then a quiet and open locality, but now at the fringe of the communal neighbourhood. In 1902 a branch of the Maz-

K

gaon school was opened in the Israel Moholla, 'the heart of the Bene Israel ghetto', for those children who found the Mazgaon school too far from their homes; this branch of the school continued until 1929. A study of the list of donors to the school building fund—Jewish philanthropists from England and France —provides a measure of the contact which Bene Israel had established with Jews elsewhere. In the 1930s Sir Elly Kadoorie, after whom the school is now named, donated some £9,000 to reconstruct the school building. To this day the school is run with a subsidy from the Anglo-Jewish Association of London and an annual grant from the Government and the Municipality.

Clearly, the Bene Israel appreciated the advantages of the school and eagerly sent their children to it. In the 1890s, when the number of Bene Israel in Bombay could not have exceeded 4,500, some 300 children—200 boys and 100 girls—attended the school. (Nowadays when the Bene Israel population in Bombay has risen to nearly 10,000, only 500 Bene Israel children attend the school.) Moreover, considering that a large number of Bene Israel children attended Missionary and Government schools, it seems that the bulk of the community's children were receiving education. Nevertheless, Kehimkar reporting on the precarious financial position of his undertaking, adds on a minatory note that unless the school receives further liberal donations some 2,000 children will be condemned to ignorance.[5]

For some years Kehimkar managed the school almost single-handed. However, it seems that as soon as he had gained the support of the Anglo-Jewish Association of London for it, he was opposed by many of his co-members. Informants said, 'Who can remember all the details of it now? But as soon as the school had become important in the community others wanted a share in its control.'

That the opposition to Kehimkar must have been very strong indeed is shown by the address with which his admirers presented him in 1900, 'That you have conferred a lasting benefit upon your community by educating their youth, and that you have with dignified calmness disregarded their aspersions. . . .' None of my informants knew for certain just why he was so strongly opposed. Perhaps it was felt that the control of the school and of a number of other enterprises on behalf of the Bene Israel gave him too much power in the community. Again, in the 1880s the first Bene

Israel university graduates appeared, and perhaps it was felt that they should take over control of the school from Kehimkar who had not received a university education—that is, the opposition to Kehimkar may have been the result of tension between the university-educated Bene Israel and the rank and file of the community.

However that may have been, the opponents of Kehimkar managed to get some members of the Anglo-Jewish Association on their side. Indeed, in 1907 a member of the council of the Anglo-Jewish Association of London travelled to Bombay, convened a public meeting of the community, and asked for suggestions about the appointment of a committee to manage the school.[6] Such a committee with Kehimkar as its president was indeed formed. Nevertheless, opposition to Kehimkar continued; and in 1909, having worked zealously for the school for over twenty-five years, he resigned. He died soon afterwards.

The work of re-organization of the school continued with great enthusiasm: the committee was invested with powers to look after and manage questions relating to education and discipline in the school; the number of children on the rolls increased by nearly fifty per cent during the first year of the committee's administration; donations from individuals increased; the synagogues of Bombay expressed their sympathy in the form of subscriptions and donations; personal service was volunteered and many a graduate acted as honorary teacher, and so on.

In the decade after Kehimkar's death the most educated members of the community both co-operated in and competed for control of the school. There were those who were mainly concerned with the standard of secular education; others complained that there was too little in the communal school to distinguish it from an ordinary school, except perhaps the substitution of Hebrew for Sanskrit as the classical language studied, and that even this teaching of Hebrew meant nothing more than the study of grammar 'and that it might have been Sanskrit or French grammar for all the difference it made to the children—there was too much concern for secular education and too little for Jewish ideals'. Although I sometimes felt that informants' concern for Jewish ideals was meant to please me rather than convey the view of the community, I did gain the impression that the principle that the school was established expressly to provide instruction in Hebrew and in Judaism over and above the ordinary school subjects was a main issue in the fight for control of the school.

From 1922 to 1951 the school had for its headmistress an unusually gifted and well-loved member of the community: of independent means, the daughter of a chief judicial officer, Bene Israel realized that she could have made a career for herself in the wider world; instead she chose to devote her working life to the welfare of the communal school. Louis Rabinowitz who visited Bombay in the early 1950s writes of her, 'To Miss Reuben I made a special pilgrimage of respect. This gracious, refined and highly cultivated lady had for years been the principal of the Bene Israel School, the Sir Elly Kadoory School. . . . She had studied at Cambridge and was to the Elly Kadoory School what the late Annie Landau was to the Evelina de Rothschild school in Jerusalem . . . the "mother" of generations of her flock. . . .'[7] She was able to address demands to her family and friends on behalf of the school; she had a much greater say in the affairs of the school than is enjoyed by her successors; certainly her presence at the school contributed to its smooth functioning.

Two members of the school committee told me, 'She was probably the most loved member of the community that anybody can remember now. But you must not think that she was not ever criticized—that would be asking too much of human nature!' And they explained that in the view of some people she was too soft-hearted to enforce 'really strict discipline'. Moreover, 'If a parent came to her and said that he could not afford to pay even the smallest fee for the education of his children, she would say "Don't worry about it: just send your children to us." It stands to reason that many people took advantage of her and that this did not help the finances of the school.' However, they admitted that Miss Reuben's own financial contributions to the school more than made up for her unwillingness to force the poor of the community to pay school fees. Again, Miss Reuben's connections enabled her to stimulate others to contribute to the funds of the school. (Thus the 1937 List of Donors cites a gift of Rs. 1,000 from the Dewan of Junagad for the Nawab Saheb. Miss Reuben's father had at one time been Chief Judicial Officer of Junagad.)

Except for those whose parents were comparatively wealthy and could afford to send their children to expensive schools, some who had won scholarships to English High Schools, and others who were brought up outside Bombay, the majority of my informants had received their education in the communal school. Indeed, many intimate friendships between co-members and some 'love' marriages appear to have been the result of contact established at the communal school. Nevertheless, although former students devote much time and energy to the welfare of the school, most of them prefer to send their children to other schools.

Nobody complained about having been unhappy at the school. On the contrary: informants who had been at the school during Miss Reuben's period as headmistress continually related incidents illustrating her kindness to pupils and her enthusiasm for teaching. Again, some Kala informants told me that after they had been teased about their descent, Miss Reuben assembled all the pupils and told them the story of King David whose great-grandmother, Ruth, had been a non-Jewess, and then added, 'Remember, even the great King David was a Kala!'[8] This incident seems to have left such an impression that on a number of occasions when there was some tension between Gora and Kala someone reminded them of Miss Reuben's teaching on the subject—but, then, as all recognized, people of Miss Reuben's class were even then much less concerned with the Gora-Kala division than the rank and file of the community.

However, it is held that the school is no longer as efficient as it used to be. And it is an indication of the low esteem in which the school is held that parents angry with their children for bringing home bad school reports may threaten them that unless they do better they will be taken away from their expensive schools and sent to the communal school. True, Bene Israel readily admit that withdrawal from the communal school results in the impoverishment of their children's Hebrew education; nevertheless, they hold that the quality of secular education is the most important consideration when choosing a school. Indeed, many Bene Israel were amazed when told that in England there is a fairly strong Jewish school movement and that some Jewish parents suffer considerable financial embarrassment in order to send their children to a Jewish school rather than avail themselves of the free and adequate schools provided by the State.

But, then, Bene Israel are now more than ever concerned about the education of their children: employment is much more difficult to come by than hitherto; in any case, a substantial part of the community is no longer content to remain clerk caste—many Bene Israel would like to see their children enter the learned professions. Again, the medium of instruction in the communal school is Marathi, and many parents fear that inadequate knowledge of English may hinder the later career of their children. (Some also held that inadequate knowledge of English may cut off their children from the more educated members of the community.) Moreover, the communal school seems to find it difficult to attract highly trained teachers. Thus the 1959 school report complains, 'Though the school is paying salaries approved by Government and Municipality, it cannot boast of a highly trained staff at present. . . . There is a tendency to use the school as a training ground for obtaining recognized educational training qualifications and then leave it for better prospects.' But I have heard it said that the main reason for the rapid turnover of staff at the school is 'too much interference from committee members —something which Miss Reuben would not have tolerated'.[9]

There is no lack of Bene Israel willing to serve on the school committee which consists of ten members elected by subscribers to the school as well as representatives of the synagogues that contribute to the school funds and of representatives of the Anglo-Jewish Association of London. I was told that Miss Reuben used to advise the Anglo-Jewish Association on whom to appoint as its representative on the school committee. During my stay in Bombay the representative of the Anglo-Jewish Association was the Headmaster of the Baghdadi school, a member of the Bene Israel community. However, the school committee no longer attracts the most illustrious members of the community. The majority of the committee's members are drawn from the rank and file, albeit from the most educated section thereof. Certainly those in prestigeful professions no longer constitute the majority; the few committee members drawn from this section are retired people with time on their hands and memories of the period when membership of the school committee was coveted and esteemed. The most sophisticated section of the community, then, no longer struggles for control of the school; its interest is expressed in frequent criticism of the school's committee and in occasional contributions to the school's funds.

Nor is it held that membership of the school committee confers great power: while membership of the synagogue committee allows one to participate in deliberations as to how to spend the income of the synagogue, membership of the school committee involves one in the difficulty of finding the finance to keep the school in existence; while the employees of the synagogue, however harassed by the committee, are unlikely to find work elsewhere, the employees of the school, if similarly harassed, will leave for better prospects; and so on. Moreover, Bene Israel no longer look upon membership of the school committee as a sign of great distinction. Indeed, while informants might be aware of and discuss in great detail the aspirations and successes (and failures) of members of the community, they would usually be unable to tell off hand whether they were also members of the school committee.

During my stay in Bombay there were 665 pupils at the school of which 269 were non-Bene Israel; the latter are drawn from the Marathi-speaking section of the children of the neighbourhood, 244 of whom pay full school-fees. A member of the school committee told me, 'The fees charged are the minimum and commensurate with the condition of the people in the vicinity. Even these fees are considerably in arrears. . . .' The school, then, is very much a charity affair; certainly nobody is exhorted to send his children to the communal school rather than to a non-communal one. 'But,' I was told by a harassed member of the school committee, 'if every parent who sends his child to a non-communal school would donate to the Bene Israel school every year only a month's school-fees which he ordinarily pays to other educational institutions for his children, the financial difficulties of our school would not be insurmountable.' And again, 'It is unfortunate that a community which can run four synagogues, two prayer-halls, a home for destitutes and orphans, a co-operative society, and a number of minor institutions, should have to look for outside help for the education of the poorer section of the community.' The school is of course the most expensive venture of the community. Nevertheless, in a recent communication I was told by someone who refuses to serve on its committee, 'The accounts of the school are in a mess. Yet with proper management it could be run without outside help.'

Nevertheless, the school seems to have established a claim

stronger than any other association on the interest and support of the community: it gets grants from the synagogues; the functions organized in its aid tend to be well attended; above all, one gets the impression that in times of great emergency it can count on the support of even those members of the community who are not normally associated with it.

Again, the money made available from non-Bene Israel sources not only supports the existence of the school but emphasizes its significance and links it to the world beyond the communal horizon. And since this is not a community turned inward but one which esteems achievements in the wider world, it is not surprising that the school, whose main object is to provide the key to advancement in that world, is generally considered to be the most important of the Bene Israel undertakings.

THE EDUCATION FUND

Efforts at educational advancement encouraged the establishment of the Education Fund by the first Bene Israel Conference in 1917. The Fund aimed at 'giving scholarships, fees and books, to deserving students (both boys and girls) in the community for Secondary, Technical, Commercial, Industrial, and Higher Education, and for giving loans to deserving students who desire to prosecute higher studies here and abroad'. It is administered by a committee elected annually by subscribers—a small group of comparatively wealthy Bene Israel, some of whom are university graduates.

One doubts whether the Fund is contributing greatly to the education of members of the community. The sum at its disposal is exceedingly small and the amount it is able to advance is tiny —one list of amounts distributed cites a grant of Rs. 10, others were less than Rs. 100. In this manner the Fund helps some half a dozen students a year with grants towards the fees for their courses.

Moreover, these grants have to be repaid; and every applicant has to provide a referee in support of the sincerity of his promise of repayment. Nevertheless, the Fund's Annual Reports contain long lists of those who have failed to repay their grants.[10] Suits have occasionally been filed against past scholars for recovery of these grants.

Not surprisingly, then, there are but few applicants for these grants. For even those who would dearly like to study realize that it would be impossible to do so on a grant advanced by the Fund unless they also have considerable financial backing from their families.

But in any case, Bene Israel lack a tradition of university education. Under the British, Bene Israel, like other minorities, such as the Christians and the Parsis and, to some extent, the Muslims, found it easy to step into jobs—the Customs, Railways, and Posts and Telegraphs were departments which were known to be the preserves of these minorities—which they could take up as soon as they completed school and which enabled them to settle down and marry early. And nowadays there is of course tremendous pressure to go to work as soon as possible.

THE HOME FOR DESTITUTES AND ORPHANS

While in England there is a feeling that it would be wrong to turn over Jewish orphans to non-Jewish agencies for, at the very least, they should be provided with food prepared in the ritual manner, an appeal by the committee of the Bene Israel Home for Destitutes and Orphans for funds because 'were it not for the Home many of our orphans would be lost to the community by conversion to other religions' fell on deaf ears. The main object of the Home is to keep Bene Israel destitutes off the streets, that is, from disgracing the community by begging. And indeed, the community numbers hardly any beggars on the streets—something of which Bene Israel are exceedingly proud. (True, when visiting a Bombay Beggars' Home I did encounter three Bene Israel inmates who had been picked up on the streets and lodged in the Home—but it was agreed that it is very rare indeed for Bene Israel to be found begging on the streets.)

It was in 1853 that Kehimkar founded The Bene Israel Benevolent Society 'for giving support to the poor and helpless widows, the supportless orphans, and the infirm men and women of the Bene Israel community'. It is said that it was one of Kehimkar's 'earliest and dearest dreams' to establish a Home for destitutes, one for which the Bene Israel Benevolent Society quietly and patiently collected funds for many years. However, it was only in 1910 that The Gate of Mercy Synagogue 'by a handsome donation, and the promise of help annually, brought the scheme down from the realm of vague dreams to the field of practical politics; in 1917 the Bene Israel Conference, by taking the project under its wings, ensured further support for it'.

Nevertheless, it was not until 1934 that the Home started functioning. There are numerous reasons for the delay. In 1907, that is, even before The Gate of Mercy Synagogue had become involved in the venture, The Bene Israel Benevolent Society purchased a plot for Rs. 15,500, having had to borrow Rs. 3,000 at interest to make up the purchase money. However, the land was required by the Bombay Improvement Trust; negotiations for the settlement of the price went on for a long time and ultimately Rs. 11,100 were awarded to the Bene Israel Benevolent Society inclusive of all interest. By 1920 a two-storeyed building had been completed; but the liabilities incurred in constructing the building made it impossible to open the Home. Later it was opened on one floor of the building, the other being let to provide an income for the Home. It now maintains some twenty orphans and six adult destitutes.

The Home is a particularly drab one. The chief reason which informants advanced in answer to the question as to why it is so neglected was that the joint household, formerly so prevalent among the Bene Israel, insured the poor and incapable against destitution. Homes for orphans and destitutes were not needed: the joint household was its own orphanage and its own home for destitutes. Thus, while admitting that if there is to be no wholesale slaughter of the incapable there must be some effort to substitute a charity organization to take over the duties of the old joint household, they argue that the existing philanthropic efforts are feeble mainly because they have not been particularly needed so far.

However, there are other factors which contribute to the neglect of the Home. Of the three partners in the venture, The Bene Israel Benevolent Society, The Bene Israel Conference, and The Gate of Mercy Synagogue, only the last still functions. Indeed, as a result of complicated High Court proceedings in 1932 and again in 1945 to remove some of the trustees on account of non-payment of their dues to the Home, The Gate of Mercy Synagogue was given authority to appoint the management of the Home. Not surprisingly, then, the Home receives a regular grant only from The Gate of Mercy Synagogue; though one of the synagogues near the Home engages the elder male orphans to swell the number of congregants at the early morning prayers, for which service it makes a small contribution to the funds of the orphanage. As it is the clerk element of the community which is in control of the synagogues, it is clerk element which is in control of the Home. Those in prestigeful professions whom one would expect to take an interest in this type of philanthropic project do not play a part in this particular venture.

Individuals will from time to time, especially on occasions of circumcision and marriage, present the inmates of the Home with a dinner, usually a chicken, to be eaten on the day on which the ritual is celebrated. And since more than one generous member of the community may celebrate such an occasion on the same day, it may happen that a long lean period is interrupted by a day of plenty. But in any case, many Bene Israel hold that the Home appears somewhat less neglected to them than to the Western visitor; indeed, an informant complained to me, 'All you Westerners are overwhelmed with horror when visiting the orphanage; you don't seem to realize that materially these orphans are not much worse off than many Bene Israel children living with their parents.' However, I have heard some Bene Israel, albeit members of the comparatively wealthy element, describe the Home as 'something out of Dickens'.

The main object of the Home—and one in which it succeeds—seems to be to keep its inmates from joining the beggars on the street—'something which would be a terrible shame to our Bene Israel community'.

THE STREE MANDAL (WOMEN'S ASSOCIATION)

This association owes its existence to one of the Bene Israel women doctors[11] who, in 1913, with the sympathy and support of her friends 'decided to encourage and bring about more friendly relations among the women of the community, to help them in improving themselves and also their more unfortunate sisters, mentally, morally and spiritually and so to fit them for their high destiny as mothers and daughters in Israel'. Its founder also sought to arrange for free medical advice and occasional monetary help for poor women and children. For the first three years the headquarters of the Stree Mandal was the Bene Israel school, but in 1916 the Mandal obtained a room of its own.

At one time the Stree Mandal held fortnightly meetings where members discussed some subject either social, religious or moral. But its main work was carried out by means of classes such as an English class, a Hebrew class, and a needle-work class. However, for many years now only the needle-work class has functioned. It is attended by some fifteen adolescent girls, some of them from the orphanage.

Indeed, the girls from the orphanage seemed especially appreciative of the needle-work class—it gave them a chance to make some new clothes for themselves—and also to escape from the Home for some hours. On the other hand, the committee of the Home seemed somewhat doubtful whether the girls should be allowed to attend the class—for there was a chance that the girls might loiter on the way and make undesirable acquaintances. In fact, one of the girls had met a member of the community in this manner, someone whom the committee considered an undesirable character, and whom she later married. Nevertheless, I was never quite sure whether the committee of the Home, drawn from the clerk element of the community, worried more about the safety of the girls in its care or about its position *vis-à-vis* the management of the Stree Mandal, that is, those in prestigeful professions—and women to boot.

The Stree Mandal, then, whose management is still in the hands of its founder, represents an attempt by the educated and sophisticated Bene Israel women to help the less fortunate women of the community. There are plans to revive the activities of the Stree Mandal. But, as informants pointed out, 'There has never been a time when Bene Israel were short of plans for forming new associations, increasing the scope of old ones, and even reviving those long since defunct!' Again, an informant, with the obvious agreement of those listening, added, 'The Stree Mandal is a place where the educated women would lecture the less educated ones —if the educated women weren't too busy in the big world and the less educated weren't too busy in their homes to come and listen.' And she then instructed me to write down: 'The goodwill is there—which is more than can be said of some other communal plans.' Thus, though the wives of the Bene Israel clerks were very much aware of the differences between themselves and the highly educated Bene Israel women, they did not engage in conflict, voiced no vehement criticism—there was just lack of contact.

THE JEWISH CO-OPERATIVE CREDIT SOCIETY

In 1918 the All India Israelite League established a co-operative store and a co-operative credit society. The store soon failed. An informant writes, 'Most ventures started at about that time failed because of lack of proper organization, being run by people with no conception of wholesale buying and no knowledge of how to decide what to stock and in what quantities.' However, the credit society, whose object it was to encourage thrift and co-operation among the Bene Israel, advancing loans on easy terms and, especially, 'to save them from the clutches of the professional money lender', survived. Indeed, for some time the society held the status of a bank; under recent legislation it has lost that status and reverted to a society since it has a working capital of less than one lakh of rupees.[12]

In the 1950s the number of members was 1,100, the number of shares was 3,346; the price of a share was Rs. 10 and the average number of shares held by a member was three. There are annual elections of committee members, but as only those holding ten shares are entitled to stand for election, it is obvious that membership of the committee of ten people is confined to a small circle.

The *Annual Reports* appeal 'to all Bene Israel Institutions and individuals to patronize the Society, the only institution of its kind in the community'. Still, there are complaints that it is difficult to become a member of the Society. Indeed, a member of the committee told me, 'I am sure our people have complained to you that it is difficult to become a member of the Society. Well, we must be careful! Our Bene Israel are poor and we must make sure that those who join are not likely to turn out defaulters.' Again, there are complaints that it is difficult to obtain a loan from the Society. On the other hand, many said that while members of the community like to own a share in the Society, they hesitate to apply for a loan—'It is like begging, a person's financial difficulties may become known in the community, and on top of it all the request will most likely be turned down.'

Indeed, informants relate that they much prefer to join small 'saving-clubs' at their place of work. These clubs, formed by friendly fellow-workers from different communities, enable members to draw on the club's funds 'in time of great expense' such as festivals. And since club members hail from different communities celebrating festivals at different times, it follows that not all of them will experience financial emergencies at the same time. Informants held that this was an excellent arrangement and not at all humiliating. In other words, Bene Israel know that savings are necessary because emergencies will occur—and that even if they are members of the Jewish Co-operative Credit Society, financial assistance will not necessarily be forthcoming.

THE BENE ISRAEL CONFERENCE AND THE ALL INDIA ISRAELITE LEAGUE

As suggested previously, both the Bene Israel Conference and the All India Israelite League represented serious attempts to establish a central body of the community.

The Conference came into existence at the suggestion of a member of the community who 'always full of ideas for communal uplift' proposed the holding of an annual meeting of Bene Israel representatives to deliberate on matters affecting the community. The idea soon caught on and the first Conference met in 1917.

However, already at the very first Conference there was a head-on collision over its scope. Arguments about the desirability of considering political questions arose as a result of an address which some eight prominent members of the Conference had presented to the Hon. Edwin Montagu (Secretary of State for India, who was touring the country in connection with the preparation of proposals for constitutional changes in India) expressing support for the scheme of reforms put forward by the Indian National Congress and the All India Muslim League. There followed an acute controversy as to whether exclusion of politics from the Conference would prevent it from considering problems affecting the community which impinged upon public affairs. However, many Bene Israel felt that the Conference should confine itself to questions affecting the internal affairs of the community and not enter upon political problems. Nor is this surprising: while some Bene Israel identified themselves wholeheartedly with the struggle for independence and the movement of Mahatma Gandhi, many Bene Israel—like many members of other minorities—sat on the fence throughout the freedom struggle.

For some years the Bene Israel Conference held regular meetings, but by 1937 it had ceased functioning altogether. Indeed, already after the first meeting of the Conference some members withdrew from it and formed a rival association, the All India Israelite League. It too soon ceased functioning.

Many of my informants hardly knew of these bodies; some, when prodded on the subject, rather irritably replied that they were not historians. A few older and more knowledgeable members of the community suggested that the only real gain to come out of it all was the decision by all synagogues to disallow polygyny—a rather severe judgement. In any case, polygyny, although nowadays exceedingly rare, is by no means completely unknown.

Though the Bene Israel Conference and the All India Israelite League had a difficult and short existence, they have some achievements to their credit. The Education Fund was started in pursuance of a resolution passed by the first Conference in 1917. The Conference also interested itself in and contributed towards the establishment of the Bene Israel orphanage. The All India Israelite League started the Jewish Co-operative Credit Society. It also considered several ambitious schemes such as the walling-in of the ancient Bene Israel cemetary in Nowgaon where, according to tradition, are buried the victims of the shipwreck from which the community dates its stay in India; a primary education fund; a hostel to be attached to the communal school; and the education of women in cottage industries. And though almost all these ambitious schemes remained completely unrealized, still, as an informant remarked, 'just thinking of them must have been good for communal uplift'.

Miss Reuben told me that whenever Jewish visitors from the West asked her, 'And what makes you think that you are Jews like us?' She replied, 'Can't you see that we are just like you? We quarrel just like you!'

Indeed, the Bene Israel situation shows striking similarities to those of other Jewish communities. As among Jewish communities elsewhere, once the first needs of the Bene Israel community were taken care of, that is, a place for worship and a place for burial, a host of subsidiary undertakings soon followed. As among Jewish communities elsewhere, these ventures frequently had a chequered career: they were hard-pressed for money and subject to conflicts. As among Jewish communities elsewhere, some of these ventures were exceedingly short-lived.

As with some Jewish communities elsewhere, there were among the Bene Israel attempts to set up rival representative bodies. As with some Jewish communities elsewhere, there was among the Bene Israel a dispute whether the school should be a secular institution, or committed to the furtherance of Judaism as well as to secular education. As with some Jewish communities elsewhere, it is the Bene Israel synagogue which is financially the most important (probably the only financially important) organization; and so forth.

It all touches a familiar chord. But there are uncommon aspects to the Bene Israel situation that also strike the observer, namely that the leadership of the community and the task of representing it to the non-Bene Israel world falls to the rank and file rather than to the most sophisticated section of the community.

Members of the community claim that it was the sophisticated section's unseemly struggle for power which deprived them of the trust of the rank and file. On the other hand, the rank and file of the Bene Israel does not consider itself incapable of dealing with the non-Bene Israel world. After all, Bene Israel have never been subjected to hostility and intolerance from the outside world and are not obsessed with the need to present themselves as exemplary citizens able to make a particular contribution to Indian life so as to defend their right to exist before the outside world. The sophisticated element of the community, being better educated and better off, are more fortunate than the rest of the community rather than more accepted by the wider world.

NOTES

1. Kehimkar, ibid. p. 160.
2. On the other hand, in a recent communication, an informant writes that there is not the same publicity to scholarships earned by Bene Israel who do not take an active part in communal affairs; and he adds that one of his nieces recently got a scholarship to Oxford.
3. B. J. Israel, ibid. p. 12.
4. Mr B. J. Israel comments on this passage, 'No! People of my generation have seen the effects in our parents and grandparents and have heard what a man like Wilson meant to the community.' (I have referred to the work of Dr John Wilson of the Scottish presbyterian Mission on pp. 40, 41.)
5. Kehimkar, ibid. p. 248. One wonders how Kehimkar arrived at this figure. In 1891 there were but 5,021 Jews in Bombay of whom about 4,500 were Bene Israel. It would be safe to assume that another 3,500 Bene Israel lived on the mainland. Thus even if Kehimkar was referring to the total Bene Israel population at that time (8,000), it is unlikely that the number of schoolchildren was 2,000. (Certainly Kehimkar's estimate of the Bene Israel population is more realistic when relating a communal quarrel in Bombay in the 1870s. In 1872 the Jewish population of Bombay was 2,669 of whom 2,300 were Bene Israel. Kehimkar, ibid. p. 256 estimates that the community then numbered some 600 or 700 hundred people—no doubt he was referring to the number of male adults only.)
6. Mr H. Landau, the member of the council of the Anglo-Jewish Association of London who travelled to Bombay to study the situation and organize the election of a committee also contributed Rs. 10,000 to the school the interest of which provides scholarships for the best pupils of the school.
7. Rabinowitz, ibid. p. 70.
8. Some informants once asked me what I thought of King David. When I replied that he was not my favourite figure in Jewish history they wondered whether I was anti-Kala. It took me some time to convince them that I objected only to his deeds and not his descent.
9. An informant writes that the last Jewish Headmistress of the school resigned in 1966 on grounds of too much interference from the committee.
10. I attended one meeting of the Fund during which applicants were interviewed; one applicant's referee proved to be one of these defaulters—which seemed a novel way of repaying a debt. Unfortunately for the applicant, the committee was neither convinced nor amused.
11. She also founded the Jewish Religious Union discussed in chapter 8.
12. Equivalent to £5,500, US $13,400.

L

10
Cliques and Clubs

Unlike the associations discussed in the previous chapter—associations purposely created for the realization of aims important to the Bene Israel such as the education of their children and the care of their orphans and destitutes—clubs tend to be the result of schoolmates and neighbours coming together in cliques and then crystallizing into organized groups either to promote an interest of their own or to supplement the work of the educational and charitable associations.

The clique is an age-graded, usually non-kin group of about half a dozen people, either neighbours and/or schoolfriends, coming together in leisure-time activities, such as playing table tennis or going to the pictures. On occasions of ritual activities in the individual life cycle which require the attendance of ten male adults, clique members will attend more readily than kinsfolk, especially on less important occasions for which kinsfolk will not trouble themselves too much. Not infrequently there develops between such a clique and a Muslim or Hindu neighbour such a close friendship that the latter participates in almost all the clique's activities. Indeed, I came across cliques whose most regular meeting place was the home of a Muslim or Hindu friend.

Sometimes it was pointed out to me that someone was not a member of the Bene Israel community—but only because it was held that this information would interest me. On one occasion I noticed that there was no *Mezuzzah* on the door of the home of the person in which the clique was meeting that evening; when I remarked upon it, I was told, 'Why should there be? He is a Hindu!' But often it would take some time before I realized that a member of the clique was not also a member of the Bene Israel community—but I am unable to decide whether this was because of lack of observation on my part or lack of differentiation on the part of the clique.

The clique is always unisexual. It would never do for Bene Israel girls to roam about as freely as do the boys—and most certainly not in the company of boys. Bene Israel say that girls found lingering about in the company of boys and chatting freely with them would damage their reputation beyond repair—'And who would offer for them then?' True, girls too may come together in friendship and, moreover they may join a club such as The Old Students' Union, the club of the former pupils of the communal school, but they have very much less free time than the boys. For girls are expected to help their mothers in the home; and as they marry early—in their late teens—they are very soon occupied with their own household affairs.

Bene Israel in their late teens and early twenties like to form clubs—they say, 'The youth of other communities form clubs: so why not Bene Israel? It gives one something to do and it is fashionable to be a member of a club.' Hence cliques turn into clubs, albeit small and short-lived ones.

Once the formation of the club is decided upon, its founders indulge in much formality such as a name and an aim and actively seek new members. Preferred names are The Sports Club or the Zionist Club and the professed aim is usually 'to help the community' by organizing functions in aid of the school, by entertaining the Bene Israel children living in the neighbourhood, and so on. Indeed, I know of two such clubs that survived long enough to arrange successful entertainments in the courtyard of a tenement for the Bene Israel children living in it. Again, one such club issued a cyclostyled bulletin for some months; and although its editor was continually complaining about lack of subscribers, it was read by many Bene Israel. The bulletin survived even the disappearance of the club; however, the editor, mistaking the mood of his readers, turned anti-Zionist at the wrong moment, and his enterprise collapsed.

Club members know one another well and what to expect of one another. For they meet practically every evening at the home of one of the members, sometimes for a short time, sometimes for hours on end. Members like to go in for sports, but having no proper facilities for it they concentrate on table tennis. There is a great demand for Jewish activities and for Zionist literature which they may obtain from the Jewish Agency-subsidized teacher in Bombay. For, in contrast to England, the Jewish State has not lost its attraction of novelty and romance; but then, many Bene Israel youth contemplate settling in Israel.

There are always projects to be discussed. A favourite topic is how to attract new members and how to convince the community of the importance of the club. For most cliques-turned-clubs dream of attracting large numbers and of arousing the interest of the community and making an impact on it. But in practice membership of the club rarely exceeds twenty. Indeed, as meetings are held in the home of one of its members, it would be difficult to accommodate a larger number; moreover, the club's short life is hardly conducive to a large membership.

For sooner or later there is some trouble over the election of office-bearers or over some project or how to go about it. Sharp words are heard—and the club passes out of existence. Some of its members, especially those unwilling to accept a position in the background, will replace it with a new one with a new name over which they can preside. Others will join an already existing one in the next tenement or in the next street.

It is not always easy to distinguish between a clique and a club. Indeed, I was associated with what seemed to be a clique for several weeks before accidentally stumbling upon the information that it considered itself a club. However, this club was rather unusual in that it had no name, and that its twenty-four members, then in their mid-thirties, intimate friends since their schooldays, would not accept new members. They explained that too many members would spoil the great friendship which existed between them and, moreover, make contact more cumbersome. Again, this club had no committee; but one of its members, an exceptionally sympathetic personality, and well-known in the community, acted as its leader.

I doubt whether many Bene Israel were aware that these twenty-four formed a club. On the other hand, they were well-known in the community as a clique of deeply attached friends, as models of devotion to communal causes, particularly to the communal school which they had all attended and where some of them had met their wives (but to which none of them sent their children), and their enthusiasm for communal work enabled them to goad indifferent individuals into activity on behalf of the community. Many Bene Israel looked upon them as prospective leaders of important communal associations.

I wondered whether they had once belonged to the Fellowship of former pupils of the communal school and left it during an especially quarrelsome period to form a club of their own. When I asked some of them about it they replied, 'It's a good guess, but we shan't tell you.' A few who knew this group said, 'What does it matter? Even if you are right, they are too old to be active members of the Fellowship now—so it all turned out for the best.'

Still, during my second visit to Bombay I found that even this club, by then of over twenty years' existence, was about to come to grief: an unmistakable coolness had replaced the former intimate friendship; clearly the club was about to dissolve. But that the club survived as long as it did is unusual. No doubt the fact that its members had been particularly close friends since childhood, the unchanging membership of the club, and the exceptionally sympathetic personality and ability of its leading figure, helped.

Most other cliques-turned-clubs break up quite quickly. And in any case, once Bene Israel have passed their late twenties, wives and children make greater demands on them—certainly more than the family in which they were born and reared tends to make on them—leaving them little time for clubs that meet most evenings. They then withdraw from club activities and fall back upon cliques once again. Each generation thus forms its own clubs anew. And each generation tends to boast of the importance its clubs had in the life of the Bene Israel community —the outings arranged, the number of children entertained, the funds raised for good communal causes, and so forth.

The first of these clubs came into being at the beginning of this century—clubs 'to discuss religion and similar subjects at weekly meetings'; clubs 'to conduct a reading room and create a circulating library on Jewish religion'; clubs 'to conduct English classes for those who cannot attend a school and Hebrew classes for those who have no opportunity to study the language of their ancestors elsewhere'; clubs 'to promote conversational meetings'; clubs 'to encourage indoor games'; clubs 'to provide means for outdoor physical exercise such as cricket, hockey and football'; clubs 'to organize *kirtans*' as a means of mass religious edification through song and connected oral exposition in prose. The composer would sing the verses alone, or with an accompanying chorus, aided by musical instruments, and would intersperse the singing with discourses which drew simple morals from the story treated or which expounded religious doctrines. The form of the *kirtan* was borrowed from the Hindus, but the theme was usually a Bible story. Mr B. J. Israel writes that a popular composer 'would attract large audiences and work them up to a pitch of emotional exaltation comparable to that worked up by a revivalist preacher. The text of the songs would often be printed and eagerly sought after, and it is possible that sometimes considerable talent went into the composition of the verses and the improvisation of the music. The institution has much declined, probably because it no longer attracts the services of *kirtankars* of the old calibre and the old unsophisticated sincerity; but even today an occasional *kirtan* is held and draws a large audience. ...'[1] Certainly one such *kirtan* which I attended in aid of the communal school moved the audience to such an extent as to promise to donate Rs. 2,600 (of which, however, only Rs. 64 were eventually handed over).

In 1909 some Bene Israel graduates formed a club which, like most other clubs, continued for some years and then disappeared from the communal scene. As informants admitted, 'The enthusiasm that is so much in evidence in the early stages soon evaporates and only few institutions have the good fortune to complete even the first decade of their existence'. Still, 1917 saw the establishment of The Israelite School Old Students' Union—probably the most important of all these clubs and, moreover, one which continues to exist albeit under a slightly different name, The Israelite School Maccabean Fellowship.

THE OLD STUDENTS' UNION

The aims of The Israelite School Old Students' Union were (1) to promote social feelings among members of the Union by conversational meetings and social gatherings; (2) to purchase books on Jewish Religion and social subjects and to study them individually or in special classes; (3) to hold debates on subjects of religious or communal interest when thought desirable; (4) to arrange for public lectures of communal interest from time to time; (5) to promote the interest of The Israelite School. An informant writes, 'The Old Students' Union which had helped the school with a large sum of money by staging the drama "The Heroism of the Maccabeans" for some reason or other stopped functioning. After every effort was made to revive it, and when it was found quite impossible to do anything further in that direction, the question arose "what next?" So a meeting was held of ex-students on 12th August 1928 at which it was decided that every school has its ex-students' union and we wanted one too. So we decided to re-name the Old Students' Union. We decided to name it The Israelite School Maccabean Fellowship. It was our wish to bind our young people to the school so that they would grow up into a sincere band of workers for it.' Informants argued that renaming The Old Students' Union was done for the sake of reviving it and that Maccabean Fellowship was an appropriate name for what it was hoped to achieve: after all, the Maccabee brothers are famous in Jewish history for their faith in the righteousness of their cause, their courage, and their distinguished acts. Moreover, one of the main periods of activity of The Israelite School Maccabean Fellowship is on Hanukkah, the popular post-biblical festival of lights celebrated in memory of the successful acts of Maccabee brothers.

Many of the activities of the Fellowship, which has some 250 members, of whom most are in their twenties (although occasionally enthusiastic older ex-students will retain their membership of the Fellowship), aim at raising funds for the school. But the Fellowship's importance cannot be measured in terms of the sums it raises for the school from time to time.

No doubt many of the members of the Fellowship—being of similar ages, following similar occupations and having similar standards of living—would in any case come together in leisure-time activities: it is only the highly educated and comparatively wealthy who spend their leisure hours beyond communal boundaries. But as a result of their preoccupation with and work for the school, the leisure hours of the old students of that school are focused on and occupied with communal affairs. Moreover, the activities organized by the Fellowship in aid of the communal school combine financial pursuits with social and religious ends.

As members of the Fellowship clearly recognize:

Hitherto Hanukkah had been a minor festival in the Bene Israel calendar, celebrated at home simply by lighting of the Hanukkah lights and giving sweets to the children. But the Hanukkah festival is associated with the story of the Maccabean heroes of old, and it is but natural that The Israelite School Maccabean Fellowship should early in its existence undertake the public celebration of the festival of Hanukkah. In 1929 we began with a one-day treat for children. Relatives and friends participated in the gaieties and everyone began to look forward to it from year to year. As the Hanukkah lights grow in number from day to day so expanded our Hanukkah celebrations which soon spread over three days. In 1944 the original Hanukkah Treat was expanded into the Hanukkah Week of today with sports, competitions, talks, entertainments. . . . Our Hanukkah celebrations have become a landmark in the community. Besides children, a great many grown-ups look forward to it. It affords opportunities for self-expression in dramatics, singing, elocution and sports. The talks are informative and interesting. The day to day celebrations bring people together in large numbers such as are seldom seen in the community. . . . The Festival has now attained great importance in the life of the community and the work of The Israelite School Maccabean Fellowship.

Again, on the Sunday after the festival of Passover the Fellowship organizes a picnic which is attended by hundreds of Bene Israel of all ages—members of the Fellowship and their families and friends. Jews look upon the day after a festival, *Isru Chag*, as not quite a weekday proper. But according to some of my Bene Israel informants it is almost a religious duty to celebrate the Passover *Isru Chag* in the form of a communal outing; and as it would be difficult to organize this on a working day, the outing takes place on the first Sunday after Passover—thus the outing has some religious significance. (It may well be that other oriental Jewish communities too celebrate *Isru Chag* in this manner and that the Bene Israel adopted it from them.)

The picnic may even be attended by non-Bombay Bene Israel; but in any case, the latter will question their friends in Bombay about the outing. The picnic involves members of the Fellowship in weeks of work—selecting a suitable site for the picnic, preparing a programme for entertainment, advertising the event on the notice boards of the various places of worship, and so on. Those charged with the cooking of the dinner will set out for the place at which the picnic is to be held as soon as the Sabbath ends and will work right through the night. Those attending the picnic will set out at dawn (and sometimes even earlier) on Sunday and only return home late at night.[2]

Sometimes such an outing proves so great a success that it will be remembered and talked about for many years. For example,

A most successful and unique occasion was the excursion enjoyed on Passover Isru Chag day in 1947. Members and friends were invited to join Moses and the Israelites in their forty years' wandering in the desert. This excursion involved much organization. The fields and woods around Chembur[3] had to be surveyed to see how far they would meet our needs. A track had to be thought out, placards prepared and set in order to mark important stages on the journey. The children had an exciting treasure hunt before they left Egypt. The excursionists crossed the Red Sea and sitting on the further bank sang songs of joy. They drank the bitter waters of Marah and ate manna of the desert. They thirsted and (aerated) water gushed forth for them out of a rock at the touch of the rod of Moses. They received the tablets of the Ten Commandments on the heights of a low mound. And when hot and tired and thirsty they grumbled against Moses, lo! the spies returned from Canaan with loads of refreshing fruit. When at last they reached the camping ground they found themselves in modern Israel in the villages of Hanitha, Birya, Kirjath Anavim and others and heard their romantic stories.

Thus did the Israelite School Maccabean Fellowship prove to its entire satisfaction that instruction can happily be combined with perfect entertainment. The excursions, besides providing opportunities for a day in the open air, for relaxation and friendship, also provide an important platform for exchange and discussion of important, living problems.

Not every picnic is oriented towards entertaining the children. Thus one picnic at which I was present was attended mainly by people in their thirties, forties and fifties who played games and recalled the past; another picnic was attended mainly by those in their early twenties who concentrated on sport and discussed the future.

Obviously, not every picnic is as well prepared or proves as great a success as the one which took place in 1947—and it is then that whatever resentment and rivalries exist between members of the Fellowship that replaced The Old Students' Union get a good chance of being aired. Then those who feel that they ought to have been consulted about the arrangements for the outing and others who may not always be on the best of terms with individual members of the current committee of the Fellowship will take the opportunity to criticize the affair. Thus on one occasion I was told, 'You can't have enjoyed that picnic! We heard it was a noisy business'; some adding, as Bene Israel are apt to do when they want to indicate that they are referring to unworthy people, 'But what can you expect of a company consisting mainly of carpenters?' Though there were some carpenters at that picnic, the majority were clerks in government and private offices or in equivalent positions; but that is neither here nor there: for Bene Israel tend to brand those of whom they disapprove as 'carpenters' —uneducated, unsuccessful, noisy and quarrelsome.

Towards the end of the 1940s some ex-students of the school, while spending a weekend at Matheran—a popular hill station not far from Bombay—'were struck with a sudden idea —"Why not a Health Home for our Bene Israel in this lovely place?"' The Fellowship took up the idea and a special committee was appointed to work it out. Informants said, 'We were ambitious and we were sustained by high hopes. We envisaged five or six small cottages, a real Health Home, where our people might seek and find rest and peace, health and happiness. And we thought not only of physical health but of mental and spiritual health as well. We visualized the Health Home as a centre for educational and recreational activities, as a rendezvous for pupils and teachers, for picnics and summer schools, for nature rambles and educational retreats. But the meagreness of the response to our appeals made our ambitions shrink to more modest dimensions.' After nearly a decade, and with the professional as well as the financial aid of some of the wealthier members of the community, the Fellowship managed to acquire a plot of land in Matheran on which it built a small cottage and a pavilion, the former to serve people of meagre means as a holiday home, and the latter to serve the needs of picnickers. Hire of the cottage and use of the pavilion is open to all Bene Israel, regardless of whether they are members of the Fellowship. It is also open to non-Bene Israel—a requirement of Government which gave the land at a concession price. But this is no hardship to Bene Israel who neither fear the non-Jew nor feel that the survival of the community requires a high degree of self-enclosure.

The inauguration weekend was attended by hundreds of ex-students of all ages, some of whom brought their wives along, as well as by some of the wealthier members of the community, especially those who had contributed to the project. The chairman of the Fellowship, a member of the clerk section of the community, stressed that the presence of those who had done well in the wider world emphasized the essential unity of the Bene Israel. Nevertheless, members of the clerk section continually drew my attention to the personality and position of those who had achieved the status of a career: 'Notice their refinement! Observe their beautiful manners!' and so on. They certainly did not seem to feel equal with those whose education and attainments involved them in a different world.

Members of the Fellowship organized the opening ceremony which included affixing the *Mezuzzah* to the doors of the cottage, and their wives prepared a festive meal. They slept in the cottage, in the pavilion, in the railway station, and spent much of the next day together walking and talking, treating the weekend as a festival of reunion. For many of them it was their first visit to a hill station, something which they had never expected to experience.

The wealthier Bene Israel stayed in hotels and only attended the formal opening ceremony; and though all knew in which of the hotels the wealthier Bene Israel were staying, they did not approach them informally or unnecessarily. For while it is true that co-membership provides a basis for an appeal for aid, it does not make for intermingling without distinction.

One of the main aims of the Fellowship is 'to promote the interest of The Israelite School'. Old students' interest is expressed mainly in raising funds for the school rather than in trying to persuade Bene Israel to send their children to it.[4] Nevertheless, as has been shown, the significance of the Fellowship is not limited to practical aspects of work for the school. For The Israelite School Maccabean Fellowship is important as a unifying force, stimulating enthusiasm for communal projects of all sorts and prodding the wealthier Bene Israel to give of their resources to these projects. Indeed, it may well be said that the activities of the Fellowship are even more valuable to the community as a whole than to the school.

Committee members are elected annually and, I am told, 'without rancour', for membership of the committee involves much expense: 'There are fares to meetings; and then when there is a function in aid of the school, committee members will spend generously.' Again, membership of the committee involves much work: indeed, many members of the committee arrange their annual leave around Hanukkah time so as to be free to organize the Hanukkah week celebrations. When I marvelled at their giving up their annual leave without much ado, they said, 'Do you mean to say that in England there would be difficulty in finding people to do this?' I said that I doubted whether any organization in England could take it for granted that its committee members would give up their annual leave to this work as a matter of course, upon which they marvelled at such selfishness. Somewhat nettled by this I pointed out that in England there was a tradition of going away on one's holiday; but as there was no such tradition among the Bene Israel of Bombay, organizing the Hanukkah Week was really a way of finding something to do during one's annual leave. However, having once come to look upon it as a generous gesture, they refused to have it argued away in this manner. Some said that they could find themselves holiday jobs which might bring in extra money; indeed, two members of the committee told me that they had turned down jobs as dancing instructors because they preferred to do the generous thing and work for the community.

In 1953 the Fellowship co-operated with the school committee in organizing a Fun Fair in aid of the school. 'Members of the Fellowship committee worked at the Fun Fair every evening from 5 till 11 or 12, and then trudged home as there were no trams or buses at that time of night, attended to their legitimate jobs during the day, and at 5 p.m. were ready again to carry on at the Fun Fair. This went on from day to day for three weeks. A drama was staged by the Fellowship during the Fun Fair, all the proceeds of which were devoted to the school.'

Still, all is not sweetness and light—among the many accounts of their work which members of the Fellowship sent me is one headed 'Disagreements':[5]

To say that we work harmoniously now is not to say that we never quarrelled. We are Maharashtrians—always at logger-heads! Things have not always gone smoothly with us. There were tiffs and bickerings, sometimes short-lived, sometimes serious. At one time the disagreements were so serious as to make us pause and think. Affairs reached a very low ebb indeed. But even in the most unsatisfactory times the Hanukkah lights kept burning throughout the Celebrations, symbolical of the unquenched light burning in the hearts of the Maccabeans. In 1944 a strenuous effort was made to re-organize the Fellow-ship. Members were asked for suggestions. Efforts were made to bring more ex-students into the fold. More scope was given to younger members so as to ensure their whole-hearted co-operation. . . . But the greatest effort was made to bring back those of our members who had broken their relationship with the Fellowship on account of internal disputes. This was very successful. Misunderstandings were removed and cordial relations established again. Though not all came back, the former bitterness was replaced by friendly feeling and the former indifference by friendly co-operation.

It must be emphasized that the phrase 'We are Maharashtrians' is an extremely rare one. I only came across it twice: in the account just quoted and, again, during the disturbances between Maharashtrians and Gujaratis over the possession of the city of Bombay when an informant told me that his sympathies and those of his wife were with the Maharashtrians 'Because Bene Israel used to live in the Konkan which is part of Maharashtra and so we are Maharashtrians.' Thus 'We are Maharashtrians' does not appear to be part of the Bene Israel myth of who they are. In the account of Fellowship disagreements just quoted, the phrase is used to explain why Bene Israel tend to be at loggerheads with each other. I do not know whether Maharashtrians are reputed to be particularly quarrelsome, but I do know that Bene Israel are conscious of frequently being at loggerheads with one an-other and frequently indulge in explanations thereof. And though no doubt in fun only, even Miss Reuben was heard to say that because Bene Israel quarrel so much, they resemble their co-religionists.

Whatever rivalries now exist within the Fellowship are of a personal character: they do not result in schisms nor do they involve the community. Though Bene Israel enjoy membership of the Fellowship committee, if not elected they appear to bear it with equanimity. For though membership of the committee can be fun, it involves much expense and hard work 'which it is not possible to carry on for very long without neglect of other duties such as wife and children'. It is my impression that such considerations lessen the strain on the working of the Fellowship.

THE YOUNG MEN AND WOMEN'S HEBREW ASSOCIATION

A small number of Bene Israel belong to a 'mixed' club, The Young Men and Women's Hebrew Association, founded by an American rabbi who, while visiting India some years ago, tried to help overcome the estrangement between Bene Israel and Baghdadis by persuading the youth of both communities to come together in social activities. As meetings of the Young Men and Women's Hebrew Association take place in the Jewish Club, a flat rented by Baghdadis for their social gatherings, some four miles from the communal neighbourhood, membership is limited to those who can afford the fares. But in any case, only the more sophisticated section of the Bene Israel youth is attracted by the club's activities such as debates and dancing.

It is certainly recognized that some members of the club hail from the most sophisticated section of the Bene Israel community. Thus on one occasion some prominent members of the community persuaded a visiting rabbi to conduct a weekend seminar for Bene Israel youth in a nearby hill station. The visitor agreed on condition that there would be a fairly large attendance, and it was suggested that the Young Men and Women's Hebrew Association was the most likely club in which a fair number of Bene Israel interested in such a project could be found. However, those involved in the arrangements demanded that they should be allowed to select the 'best people' from those interested in attending the seminar; (to its credit) the committee of the club refused to subject its members to rejection and the seminar did not take place. The incident illustrates the position of the club: its members tend to be drawn from the most sophisticated section of the community, but it is nevertheless too democratic to be exclusive.

Baghdadi members are few in number and tend to be drawn mainly from the poorer section of their community. The more affluent Baghdadis fear that membership of the club may involve their offspring in too much contact with Bene Israel and with the poorer section of their own community. Occasionally, however, a particularly attractive project will bring some of the more affluent Baghdadi youth to the club—with or, sometimes, without the knowledge of their parents.

There are a few affluent Baghdadi members, in their late twenties, and it is my impression that they tend to look upon their membership of the club as some sort of social work—organizing social activities for the poorer members of their own community and helping to Judaize the more affluent and sophisticated section of the Bene Israel youth, that is, setting an example of Orthodoxy, introducing them to Jewish customs and habits, and by friendly contact supporting them in their efforts to become an integral part of the Jewish people. (Two of these older, affluent Baghdadi members with whom I discussed this point confirmed my impression, admitted that they enjoyed the task they had set themselves, but refused to consider that it was perhaps an unnecessary task, and that in any case Bene Israel were a part of the Jewish people.)

Within this club members of both communities get on well together; again, members of both communities make up the committee. In fact, one gets the impression that there is a strong desire on the part of members of each community to 'appear well' before the other and, moreover, to set an example to Bombay Jewry. Indeed, the club makes an annual donation to the Bene Israel school. I do not know whether the club also makes an annual donation to the Baghdadi school; but in any case, the latter enjoys much greater financial resources than does the Bene Israel school.

Still, during my last visit to India I was told that this club too is about to dissolve: informants said that it had been in existence for so long that every subject had been debated upon and even dancing had lost its attraction. Above all, so many members were emigrating that it was much too difficult to keep the club going.

As is the case with the Bene Israel educational and charitable associations, Bene Israel cliques and clubs touch a familiar chord. As among Jews in the West, cliques of young Bene Israel turn into clubs: it is the thing to do and also fun. As among Jews in the West, sometimes the initial enthusiasm soon evaporates, sometimes quarrels bring about rapid dissolution. As among Jews in the West, some Bene Israel clubs, such as sports clubs, parallel those in the wider world, while others have specifically Jewish aims, such as to discuss Jewish principles and to perform useful work for this Indian Jewish community. As among Jews in the West, the form of Bene Israel activities may be borrowed from the wider world, but the content is Jewish. For example, as the Anglo-Jewish minister is dressed in the garb of the Christian clergyman while preaching the meaning of Judaism to his congregation, the form of the Bene Israel *kirtan* is borrowed from the Hindus, while the content is taken from the Bible. As among Jews in the West, when Bene Israel get older they tend to withdraw from club activities and fall back upon cliques once again, and so the process goes on.

But there are differences. Thus, in contrast to Jews in the West, all Bene Israel cliques and virtually all Bene Israel clubs are unisexual: neither cliques nor clubs are groups which Bene Israel join to find marriage partners. It is true that among strictly Orthodox Jews in the West too cliques and clubs tend to be unisexual. But even to the strictly Orthodox Jews from the West who live long enough among the Bene Israel to get to know the habitual goings-on among them, the relations between the sexes must appear startlingly restrained. Moreover, it is my impression that Bene Israel clubs are somewhat more religious in aim than many Jewish clubs in the West—Judaism has not lost its interest for Bene Israel nor do they take their membership of Jewry entirely for granted. But they do take their communal existence for granted: hence there is no objection to nor apprehension of non-Jews participating in the activities of Bene Israel cliques and clubs. It is only during prayer time that Bene Israel insist on complete self-enclosure.

Perhaps it is this feeling of security in the continued existence of the community that accounts for the equanimity with which they face the failure rate of their clubs. Clubs are fashionable and fun, but Bene Israel do not fear that without them they will lose their youth. It is notable therefore that the Maccabean Fellowship should have continued for so long. But it is not surprising. For the Fellowship is involved in an association which to the Bene

Israel is next in importance to the synagogue—neither synagogue nor school must be allowed to disintegrate.

But in spite of their short life, there is more to these clubs than fashion and fun: they are important. For they help to confine the excitement which people seek in their leisure-time within communal boundaries. Moreover, in a community which does not provide a training centre for communal leaders, clubs are training grounds for those willing to take upon themselves communal responsibility. And no doubt those most involved in club activities will one day find themselves among the leaders of the community: years of devotion will not remain unrecognized.

NOTES

1. B. J. Israel, ibid. p. 12.
2. Much as I enjoyed these outings, they proved to be exercises in physical endurance.
3. Chembur is a suburb of Bombay. It is also the place in which Miss Reuben, then headmistress of the school and President of the Fellowship, lived. In fact, the project was her idea.
4. In the previous chapter I referred to the low esteem in which the school is held.
5. As pointed out in the Introduction, members of the community continually sent me long accounts of their views and doings.

M

11
Conclusion

The subject of many of the preceding chapters has been the sphere that marks out Bene Israel social life, the way in which this Indian-Jewish community keeps itself intact.

It is comparatively easy to recognize similarities between the Bene Israel and Jewish communities elsewhere: the critical institutions, that is, those that support religious life, exist everywhere, whether the community is situated in Berlin, Birmingham, Baghdad or Bombay, and without them the community would cease to be Jewish as Jewishness is usually and traditionally understood.

It is also comparatively easy to recognize a striking difference between the Bene Israel community and many other Jewish communities: Bene Israel, because of their long isolation from the main stream of Jewish life, lack a tradition of Jewish learning. Nor did they ever experience a situation in which Jewish scholarship, and descent from distinguished Jewish scholars, was the basis of highest prestige. They have among them not even a tiny minority for whom the life and study of Judaism constitutes the main purpose of living. They do indeed appreciate learning, they covet and esteem it; but it is the learning to be gained only in the wider world, and their status system is a replica in miniature of what exists in the wider world, lacking the complexity peculiar to the status system of many other Jewish communities.

Again, it is comparatively easy to recognize that the position of the Bene Israel community, which has nestled for so long in the shadow of the Indian caste system, differs from that of many other Jewish communities. For the caste system allows any community to be fitted as a co-operating part of the social whole *and* to retain its own character and its separate individual life. The Bene Israel do not form a minority *par excellence* in the country in which they find themselves. They have no fear for their communal survival, nor do they feel the need to justify their community's existence. And it may well be that it is this factor which accounts for the comparative equanimity with which they face the failures of many of their communal undertakings.

In contrast to other Jewish communities, where earlier arrivals form a sort of aristocracy, there is no social differentiation between the Bene Israel on the basis of time of arrival in India. For whether or not every single member of the community wholeheartedly believes in the tradition of descent from members of the Ten Lost Tribes who were shipwrecked off the Konkan on the west coast of India some two thousand years ago, and whether or not in fact the Bene Israel community owes its origin to more than one immigration, I have never heard of anyone who doubted that the community owes its origin to one immigration. But in any case, all Bene Israel are equally familiar with the language and customs of the part of India in which they find themselves, all are equally able to deal with non-Bene Israel in their everyday affairs —all are equally Indian Jews. And it may well be that it is this equality *vis-à-vis* the wider world which enables them to face with equanimity the fact that they are represented to the wider world by the clerk element rather than by those of their members who are distinctly superior in education and occupation. Bene Israel have no need to point to the contributions of those of their members who are superior in achievements in order to plead their right to citizenship.

If there is confusion about the Bene Israel, if they are a puzzle to others and sometimes even to themselves, it is not in relation to their fellow Indians but to their fellow Jews. It is the latter who ask 'Who are the Bene Israel?'

This is not a propaganda pamphlet, and I am not concerned with the question whether the Bene Israel are Jews, a question which strikes me as both unwarranted and distasteful, but which has received extensive and continuous publicity. What seems to me worth asking is why the question should have arisen. What is it that is puzzling and challenging about the Bene Israel?

Physically and in their circumstances the Bene Israel appear different from their fellow Jews. There are reasons for the difference.

Though many Jews tend to think of themselves, and many non-Jews tend to think of them, as a race, they are not physically a homogeneous group, but approximate everywhere to the people among whom they have been living for centuries. Not all Jews are Europeans.

However, the number of the Bene Israel is so small, and they have been living for so long on the outer rim of Jewish life, that they almost inevitably escaped notice. Once 'discovered' they were found to resemble in colour and customs the people of India—a people not usually associated with Jews and Judaism—*and* a subject people into the bargain.

The comparatively fair-complexioned Baghdadi Jews had at first freely used Bene Israel synagogues and cemeteries. But after many of them took to a European mode of life, and particularly after their leaders were accepted in British society, they began to regard themselves as different from their Indian co-religionists. They began to isolate themselves, suggesting that 'pure Jewish blood' does not flow in the veins of the Bene Israel.

Many Bene Israel appear to have felt patronized by these newcomers and, worse, considering the contempt in which the half-caste was held, feared for their status in the eyes of their fellow Indians. Clearly the conflict has lost much of its significance in the changed social climate of contemporary India. But the conflict has not disappeared: it had been brought to the notice of Jewry abroad, particularly in Israel, where, for a time, it was waged with renewed vigour, this time not on the grounds of the purity of the Bene Israel blood, but on the validity of their marriage customs.

Why have so many Bene Israel gone to Israel? They were not in complete ignorance of the possibility of friction between Jewish communities differing widely in colour, custom, education, occupation, wealth and influence.

After all, Bene Israel enjoy all the privileges of Indian citizenship. Persecution is known to them only from hearsay; they have never experienced it. They have lived for many centuries on excellent terms with Hindus, Muslims, and Christians.

There has, however, been a decline of confidence. As one member of the community who describes himself as a 'detached observer' of the problem put it:

Among all the good, bad and indifferent things the British did, one with perhaps the most painful after-effects is the privileged position they gave to the smaller religious minorities. Like the Christians and Parsis, and, to some extent, the Muslims, we found it easy to step into petty jobs in offices and workshops. . . . 1947 changed all that. We were put on our mettle. We had to compete on the basis of pure merit. Perhaps, here and there, communalism does operate to the detriment of candidates without push or influence, but, by and large, our young men and women just lack the grit and determination for survival in a harsh environment. . . . Many of our people have come to believe that, as Jews, their first loyalty should be to Israel. . . . They expect that Israel will prove as indulgent a parent as the India of British days. As for me, I'm for India—first, last and always. . . .

The prospects appeared bright: while the Baghdadis did not regard the Bene Israel as 'pure Jews', the Israeli representatives —all of whom were (or were believed to be) of European origin— made no such distinction. In the Israeli Consulate and in the offices of the Jewish Agency Bene Israel and Baghdadis were treated alike. Hence Bene Israel assumed that common religion would provide a framework for easy social relations with European Jews in Israel. And it is significant that many Bene Israel prepared themselves for migration not only by acquiring the rudiments of the Hebrew language but also by trying to increase and deepen their knowledge of the principles and practices of Judaism. Moreover, though it would be untrue to speak of the magnet of Zionism or messianic longings, there was nevertheless a definite wish on the part of many Bene Israel to link themselves to a Jewish State in the Holy Land.

However, the directive requiring an investigation 'as far back as is possible' of the ancestry of the Bene Israel contemplating marriage with members of other communities of Jews became a new source of resentment. Once again the Bene Israel were in the news. Whatever the religious merits of the marriage controversy—and it is my contention that it need never have arisen had more been known about Indian Jewry—to many Bene Israel it appeared to be a continuation of the issue of racial purity, of the recurring question 'Who are the Bene Israel?'

The case of the Bene Israel is singular because of its Indian context; factors such as caste and the backwash of British rule have contributed to the problem. Nevertheless, the question raised in connection with the Bene Israel of India reflects the problems posed by the many divisions and subdivisions of Jewry—contributing to the preoccupation with the problem of 'Who is a Jew?'

Bibliography

ASUBEL, N. *A Treasury of Jewish Folklore*, New York, 1948.

BAILEY, F. G.
  (1) *Caste and the Economic Frontier*, Manchester, 1957.
  (2) *Tribe, Caste, and Nation*, Manchester, 1960.

BENJAMIN, I. J. *Eight Years in Asia and Africa*, Hanover, 1863.

BRIGGS, L. C. and GUÉDE, N. L. *No More For Ever: A Saharan Jewish Town*, Cambridge, Mass., 1964.

BUCHANAN, C. *Christian Researches in Asia*, London, 1811.

DAVIS, M. 'Centres of Jewry in the Western Hemisphere', *Jewish Journal of Sociology*, V, 1, pp. 4–26, 1963.

DUMONT, L. and POCOCK, D. F. *Contributions to Indian Sociology*, Nos. 1, V, VI, Paris.

EZEKIEL, M. *History and Culture of the Bene Israel in India*, Bombay, 1948.

FIRTH, R. *Elements of Social Organization*, London, 1961.

FREEDMAN, M. *A Minority in Britain*, London, 1955.

GODBEY, A. H. *The Lost Tribes: A Myth*, Duke University Press, 1930.

GOITEIN, S. D. 'Jewish Education in Yemen as an Archetype of Traditional Jewish Education' in Frankenstein ed. *Between Past and Future*, Jerusalem, 1953.

HUTTON, J. H. *Caste in India*, London, 1951.

ISRAEL, B. J. *Religious Evolution among the Bene Israel of India Since 1750*, Bombay, 1963.

KEHIMKAR, H. S. *The History of the Bene Israel of India*, Tel-Aviv, 1937.

KODER, S. S. 'The Jews in Malabar'. *India and Israel*, Bombay, 1951.

LEACH, E. R.
  (1) *Political Systems of Highland Burma*, London, 1954.
  (2) *Aspects of Caste in South India, Ceylon, and North-West Pakistan*, Cambridge, 1960.

MANDELBAUM, D. G. 'The Jewish Way of Life in Cochin', *Jewish Social Studies*, New York, 1939.

MARRIOTT, McK. 'Interactional and Attributional Theories of Caste Ranking', *Man in India*, XXXIX, 2, 1959.

MAYER, A. C.

(1) *A Report on the East Indian Community in Vancouver*, Working Paper, Institute of Social and Economic Research, University of British Columbia, 1959.

(2) *Caste and Kinship in Central India*, London, 1960.

PARKES, J. *A History of the Jewish People*, London, 1964.

PEREYRA DE PAIVA, *Notisias dos Judeos de Cochim*, Amsterdam, 1686.

RABINOWITZ, L. *Far East Mission*, Johannesburg, 1952.

SHAFER, B. C. *Nationalism: Myth and Reality*, London, 1955.

SAMUEL, S. *A Treatise on the Origin and Early History of the Beni-Israel of Maharashtra State*, Bombay, 1963.

SRINIVAS, M. N.

(1) *Religion and Society among the Coorgs of South India*, Oxford, 1952.

(2) 'The Social System of a Mysore Village' in Marriott ed. *Village India*, Chicago, 1955, pp. 1–35.

(3) *Caste in Modern India*, London, 1962.

STRIZOWER, S.

(1) 'Jews as an Indian Caste', *The Jewish Journal of Sociology*, London (Vol. 1, No. 1), 1959.

(2) *Exotic Jewish Communities*, London, 1962.

(3) 'The Jews in India', *New Society*, London, 9 January 1964.

(4) 'The Bene Israel in Israel', *Middle Eastern Studies*, London II, 2, January 1966.

WILSON, J.

(1) *Lands of the Bible*, Bombay, 1847.

(2) *Appeal for the Christian Education of the Bene Israel*, Bombay, 1866.

Index

All India Israelite League, 128, 130, 143, 144–5

Anglo Jewish Association, London, help to Bene Israel school, 41, 71–2, 130, 131, 132, 133, 136

Appeal for the Christian Education of the Bene Israel, 15, 170

Aspects of Caste in South India, Ceylon and North West Pakistan, 169

Asubel, N., 80n.4, 169

Avalaskar, S. V., 22, 31n.1, 32n.8

Baghdadis, *see* Jews in India from Baghdad

Bailey, F. G., 22, 169

BENE ISRAEL
absence of political involvement, 72–3, 144–5
absence of priests as evidence of mixed descent, 68–9
admission to Baghdadi schools, 69, 80n.7, 80n.8
adoption of name, 18–19n.6, 32n.7
age of marriage, 86–7
alleged discovery by brother of Moses Maimonides, 35–6
armed forces, service in, 24, 33n.19, 39, 49n.10, 99–100
arranged marriages, 86–8
arrival of David Rahabi, 35
attendance at non-Jewish schools, 77, 129, 132, 134–5, 136, 137
Baghdadi attempts to establish difference from, 44–7, 62n.4
caste characteristics, 9, 22, 26–7, 31, 39, 49n.12
cemeteries in Bombay, 75, 115, 128
Charity Fund, 58, 119

circumcisions, 113–14
claim to distinctive physiognomy, 54–5, 62n.2
cliques and clubs, 8, 148–52, 161–2; participation of non-Jews, 148–9, 162
colour of indication of ethnic purity, 27–8, 46
communal neighbourhood, 59, 110, 126n.2
contemporary households, 100–2, 108n.15
controversy about acceptability for marriage, 4, 47–8, 95–6, 166, 167
cooperative credit society, 75, 78, 82n.19, 130, 143–4, 145
descent from the Ten Tribes, 5, 10, 12–13, 15, 16–17
description as 'clerk caste', 39, 77; as 'Jew caste' or 'Israel caste', 40, 49n.12
divergence from Jewish image, 9, 48, 55, 56, 126, 164, 165–6
divorce among, 96
dress, 55, 56, 62–3, 63n.6; as separating factor from Baghdadis, 55
eating of beef, 24–5
economic condition, 75–9
Education Fund, 58, 130, 138–9, 145
educational progress, 40–1, 129, 132, 147n.2
efforts for uplift in later 19th and early 20th centuries, 128–9
egalitarianism, 76, 165
employment of Baghdadi priests, 67–9
ethnic purity, 4, 16–17, 23, 44, 46, 50n.18, 68, 167

25.)